ANCIENT WISDOM

AND

MODERN MAN

CW00818981

ANCIENT WISDOM
AND
MODERN MANAGEMENT

JAGDISH KUMAR

UBS Publishers' Distributors Ltd.

New Delhi ● Bombay ● Bangalore ● Madras ●
Calcutta ● Patna ● Kanpur ● London

UBS Publishers' Distributors Ltd.
5 Ansari Road, New Delhi-110 002
Bombay Bangalore Madras
Calcutta Patna Kanpur London

© Jagdish Kumar

First Published 1994

Cover Design : UBS Art Studio

Typeset at UBSPD in 11 pt New Century Schoolbook
Printed at Rajkamal Electric Press, Delhi

**To
Lord Krishna**

Preface

During the vast span of recorded history, all great religions of the world have been involved in wars at some point of time or the other. These wars have been chronicled in religious texts such as the Mahabharata, the Ramayana, the Bible and the legends of the Sikh Gurus. These texts have not only described the various struggles between right and wrong but have also elaborated upon the righteous conduct for humans. In the present-day context, it should be emphasized that many of the modern management principles have primarily evolved from learning gleaned from wars and battles on land, sea and air.

Over the centuries, grandparents, parents and other relatives and later the 'gurus' provided fascinating accounts (in the form of learning inputs), for children, of these titanic battles and the correct codes of behaviour. The modern life styles, for a variety of reasons (not the least due to the 'entertainment invasion' by satellite TV and by the almost ubiquitous VCR/VCP), have deprived the young ones of these value-building inputs.

Over the years my desire to correlate modern management principles to religious texts grew. This was to provide exposure of religious texts to the young, as also to help them simultaneously absorb modern management principles in a simple way. The fifty stories contained in this volume have been selected from various religious sources. These stories merely touch the fringes of the vast world of wisdom included in the religious texts. The 'age of communication' is constantly making the world grow smaller; for individuals to succeed in such an environment they need to be exposed to these fundamentals of management at the earliest possible opportunity.

This book is aimed not only at students but also at working women and men, irrespective of their field of endeavour. Any situation only modifies the degree of emphasis to be placed on different fundamentals at different times – the basic principles, *per se*, do not change. All individuals, besides carrying the burden of accountability in their work situations, also play an important role in their families and society; the aforementioned principles are totally extendable to all these environments. The leaders of the future are being increasingly moulded in schools and colleges, as class monitors, captains of sports teams, or leaders of extracurricular activity groups or social organisations like Rotaract and Scouts and Guides. They, as much as anybody else, need to understand, apply and internalise these principles.

In this book the following *italicized* words have been used as totally interchangeable:

(1) *Manager / leader / top management / boss*: Each one has a vital role to lead a group to continued growth and success. Management has six resources: four M's (men, machines, material, and money) and two T's (time and technology). The word 'manager' is to be read as 'manage-r, i.e., one who manages resources. 'Leader' is to be read as 'lead-e-r', i.e., 'lead in effective use of resources.' The top management only represents a group of high ranking managers.
(2) *Organisation / company / industry / group*: Each word only indicates an organised activity with a commonality of goals.
(3) *Effective / objective*: Both these words relate to the achievement of desired results on the basis of logical analysis of a situation/problem.

For easily correlating different parts of the ancient story to various management learning dimensions, the paragraphs have been numbered identically; i.e., para 1 of the ancient story corresponds to para 1 of the management concepts, and so on.

Light reading can be enjoyable if coupled with learning; the impact, invariably, wears off with time. However, if such reading leads to introspection and to subsequent situation-

dependent application to any facet of life, it has a life-long
effect. The underlying fervent hope is that this book will be
read and applied to real-life situations; even a few readers
practising the principles given here would amply reward my
efforts.

Pune   **Jagdish Kumar**

Acknowledgements

First of all, umpteen thanks to my friends and colleagues: Mr F.J. Dastoor, Mr P.S. Doctor and Mr P.M. Khanchandani (all of Poonawalla Group of Companies, Pune) for motivation and unstinted support.

My gratitude to Mrs Bharati Mulchandani for insightful comments, patience and converting my scribbles into readable material.

Contents

Part V: Sikhism

Part VI: Christianity and Judaism

Part VII: Sufism

Part I

Lord Krishna

1. Guru Dakshina (Offering to the Guru)
(The Ancient Story)

1. Lord Krishna, when ready to receive training in different sciences and arts, was sent to the ashram (residential institution) of Sage Sandipani. Lord Krishna was tireless, brave and polite. He would gladly do all sorts of odd jobs around the ashram, such as bringing firewood from the forest and milking the cows. Sage Sandipani enjoyed grooming Lord Krishna, who was not only an eager student but also a fast learner. The wisdom and knowledge acquired at the ashram constituted the solid foundation for future learning.

2. After the training was completed, Lord Krishna asked the sage as to what could he offer as a token of his gratitude and respect. Sage Sandipani requested that his son, who had been taken away by the demons, be rescued. Shri Krishna attacked the demons and returned the son to Sage Sandipani.

The Related Modern Management Concepts

1. The ancient concept of the 'guru' (teacher) is extremely powerful. In the present context, a 'boss'/manager occupies that position for all practical purposes. No employee can totally separate his/her work life from his/her personal life—factors such as the successes, failures, problems, pressures and demands related to one always infringe upon the other. An individual invariably carries the domestic exigencies along to his/her job, which has a direct impact on his/her work output. Abilities, attributes, values and knowledge, which help an individual solve different kinds of problems are common; their *application* varies from one situation to another. The manager should objectively assess the various facets of an individual and should then undertake training and counselling of that individual. Such guidance should aim at strengthening the individual, through continuous self-development, to effectively cope with the wide variety of problems thrown up by life. The imparting of knowledge should be a planned, time-bound activity. The long-term aim should be to develop a grasp of diverse subjects such as functional management, general management, behavioural sciences and socio-economic and political factors which make an impact on the business environment. The subordinates should be helped to internalise the need for learning in one's self-interest. A burning desire to succeed, once kindled, will result in the automatic forthcoming of appropriate effort.

2. The manager should have no expectation of a *dakshina* (fees) from his subordinates in monetary or material terms and, if offered should tactfully decline acceptance. Also, the subordinates should not offer such gifts; the subordinates should instead repay the 'guru', by demonstrating loyalty, application of knowledge, undertaking self-development and, above all, objectively sharing their successes and failures with the 'boss' to further their learning. The subordinates should have the courage to express their perceptions/views even if contrary to those of their manager, in a logical and resolute manner. Such behaviour will develop boss-subordinate emotional bonds and consequently strengthen the team.

NUGGETS

- The manager must be like a 'guru'. By developing strong, competent and reliable subordinates, the manager becomes available for conceptualising and planning newer and more ambitious projects.
- Self-development alone can ensure future growth and success.
- A consistent improvement in performance is the finest *Dakshina* a subordinate could offer to his manager.

2. Sudama and His Rice Flakes
(The Ancient Story)

1. Lord Krishna and Sudama studied together, for a long time, in the same ashram. Their backgrounds were diverse; Lord Krishna hailed from a royal family and Sudama from a poor Brahmin family. They immensely enjoyed each other's company and developed deep bonds of friendship.

2. Over the years, Sudama remained very poor. In sheer helplessness, Sudama got persuaded by his wife to go and meet Lord Krishna, his old friend, now the king of Dwarka. Sudama did not want to take undue advantage of his old friendship and ask Lord Krishna for something; however, very reluctantly, he set out on his journey.

3. Sudama was given a small packet of rice flakes by his wife, as a present for Lord Krishna – that is all that they could afford.

4. Sudama could not gain entry into the palace, since the guards were unaware of Sudama's old relationship with Lord Krishna. However, when Lord Krishna was told of the arrival of a poor Brahmin called Sudama, he personally came out to the gate and took him into the palace.

5. Lord Krishna saw Sudama hiding the small packet of rice flakes; he understood that it was a gift for him and forced Sudama to hand it over. Lord Krishna happily accepted the rice flakes and ate some.

6. Sudama returned home, having asked for nothing. However, on reaching home, he found a large house instead of his hut, awaiting him, and his family members enjoying the benefits of riches and wealth (bestowed, obviously, by Lord Krishna).

1. Emotional bonds develop with long association, and through sharing of common living conditions, joys and adversities. In organisational life, people come together from diverse backgrounds for varying periods of time, at different hierarchical levels, at times having authority relationships. Therefore, special efforts must be made to develop emotional bonds amongst people, in a compressed period of time. Effective use of *team-building techniques* knits people together emotionally, since they jointly enjoy the successes and share the adversities. The desire to cooperate and extend oneself to help other individuals accrues from team spirit; which, in turn, results from the existence of such bonds.

2. On certain occasions, one-time old associates may have problems in life and be shy of seeking help. Organisations which keep in touch with such old associates, and extend reasonable support without being asked, build up a very positive image in the employment market. Talented people join and remain in such organisations, since they appreciate the power of emotional bonds.

3. Often, presents are exchanged by different levels of employees amongst themselves and with those outsiders who are business associates. In all such cases, the spirit and affection behind the act must be understood, which are critical factors; the money value of the present is a minor issue.

4. The successful persons in industry should model their behaviour on Lord Krishna. The riches of a person are less important than the emotional attachments; old associates must be recognised and made honoured guests. A gesture of this kind would enhance the personal respect for the leader amongst the followers.

5. It is not always feasible to give expensive presents on occasions such as marriages, anniversaries or birthdays. At times, colleagues and subordinates shy away from participating in such personal events, because of the inability to buy an appropriate gift. Organisational culture must remove such dilemmas, by setting good precedents. The family feeling generated by participation in personal events is irreplaceable.

---

6. Organisations can extend help in discreet ways, without hurting the 'self-esteem' of the receiver. The top management can better understand the needs of employees by personal interactions in an informal atmosphere. Needs, if possible, met without asking, increase the emotional bonding and, hence, the loyalty of the employee.

NUGGETS

- 'Equivalent affluence' forms a weak base for friendships.
- Emotional bonding has to be 'made to happen'.
- Team spirit results from emotional bonding.

3. Lord Krishna and Goverdhan
(The Ancient Story)

1. The people of Gokul, as a custom, always thanked Lord Indra (lord of heaven) after a good monsoon. Goverdhan was a mountain situated near Gokul, where grass grew in large quantities. Lord Krishna and his friends grazed their cattle on Goverdhan and also played out there. The cattle got enough grass to eat and yielded large quantities of milk.

2. One particular year, after a good monsoon, Lord Krishna suggested to his friends that they worship Goverdhan instead of Lord Indra, since it was the mountain which provided food for the cattle which, in turn, gave them milk, curds, butter, and other related products. Therefore, a big festival was held to worship Goverdhan.

3. Lord Indra got annoyed at this behaviour and sent down heavy rains to flood Gokul. Lord Krishna instilled courage in the frightened people and assured them that Goverdhan would take care of them. Shri Krishna led all the people, along with their cattle to the mountain, and lifted Goverdhan on his small finger. Goverdhan sheltered all of them for seven continuous days till God Indra realised his folly and stopped the rains. The people of Gokul thereafter treated Lord Krishna as their god.

1. Work and play can be combined. Such a combination not only gets the work done quicker but also keeps people motivated to perform to even better standards. Expression of gratefulness for rewards received fosters emotional harmony between the management and the employees. Such an expression should reflect genuine feelings and not be a false show or a manipulative activity.

2. The top management must remain visible down the line to all the employees. The impact of their personalities must keep getting renewed. Otherwise, the intermediate levels of management are perceived as all-powerful and givers of rewards. In such a situation, the top management loses touch with ground reality and, psychologically, employees regard them as 'outsiders'.

3(a). Decisions should not be taken when one is angry or in a state of mental turmoil. At such times, emotions overrule logic and distort reality. In adverse conditions the leaders need to remain cool and calculating; they should reassure their people through personal interaction and persuasion. The chosen course of action should be clearly explained to give unidirectional thrust from each team member. The top management must show genuine concern for setting things right by visible acts, especially in times of trouble or uncertainty. Leaders must go ahead and act first; then people will follow. It is necessary to correctly evaluate the strength of the opposite party. Any miscalculation will lead to a loss. It would be wise to negotiate and arrive at an amicable understanding.

3(b). The duration of adverse periods can be long; however, patience and persistence are required to win finally. Those outsiders who wish to harm the organisation can have only limited effect, if all persons combine and fight back like a team. Successful top leaders become objects of great respect, amongst the team members, when they achieve spectacular success. This process has to be an ongoing one and not a one-shot endeavour.

NUGGETS

- Rewards must be given on visible performance.
- The top management must remain visible and should lead by personal example.
- Team spirit has to be built up and nurtured.
- Cohesive teams win the final battle.

Part II

Mahabharata

4. King Bharata
(The Ancient Story)

1. The first, and one of the most famous and powerful kings amongst the Kauravas, was Dushyant. He was married to Shakuntala. Shakuntala carried a curse of Sage Durvasa and, as a consequence thereof, was separated from her husband after a short time together. During this separation, Shakuntala lived in the forest, where Bharata was born. Bharata, as a young child of four years or so, was quite content playing with tigers, panthers and other wild animals. It has been rightly stated that 'coming events cast their shadow'. Shakuntala saw in her son the qualities of his father and a great king in the making.

2. The curse of Sage Durvasa had run its course and lost its effect. Dushyant and Shakuntala were united and returned to former's palace. Dushyant expanded his territories and established a powerful kingdom. One day Bharata ascended the throne. He proved greater than all others in bravery, wisdom, looking after his people and religious practices. He initiated democracy as a way to govern his kingdom. He carved out a huge, powerful, prosperous empire and earned the title of *'Chakravarti Samrat'* (Supreme Emperor).

3. At the appropriate time Bharata consulted the royal priests and appointed a successor from outside his family – he acted on the belief that a son may not be gifted like his father, and, therefore, may not prove to be a capable and successful king. He placed the interests of his people and kingdom far above his own sentiments and feelings.

1. Entrepreneurs have certain special attributes which enable them to be pioneers, chart out new paths, overcome unforeseen obstacles and achieve success. These qualities, if cultivated in the managers, will make them more versatile, dynamic, result oriented and better decision-makers. Organisations need to identify these qualities, objectively evaluate their managers and through counselling, coupled with planned management development inputs, convert them into 'intrapreneurs'. Young entrants into any organisation bring a breath of fresh air. Such entrants are not yet inhibited by past practices and traditions; are prepared to experiment and take risks; are curious to acquire knowledge; and are fired with a burning desire to succeed. These qualities need to be nurtured for strengthening the organisation in order to effectively cope with the uncertainties of the future. The talented individuals should be identified early and placed for grooming under managers, who possess 'guru' attributes.

2. Periods of adversities and of good fortune are cyclical in nature; they come and go. It is a test of true leadership to reduce the adverse periods to the minimum possible. Adversity offers a great opportunity for learning; it throws up organisational weaknesses, whether they be in policies, systems, procedures, people management, product updating, diversification thrust and so on. Moaning and groaning during adversity produce a ripple effect and drown practically everybody in a sea of frustration. The top management has the onerous responsibility of ensuring continued growth and enhancement in the profitability of the organisation. All the management resources (men, machines, money, material, time and technology) must be harnessed in a mutually interdependent mode. This calls for a great degree of alertness in setting targets, monitoring performance and initiating timely remedial action as and when appropriate. Fair and value-based policies, ruthlessly implemented, go a long way in achieving success.

---

3. Management succession is a delicate and sensitive issue, primarily in dynastic organisations. The top management has a right to train, groom and prepare the younger family members to sit at the helm of affairs one day. However, organisational interests must override personal and family demands, by having only the meritorious and capable succeed the top man. Family members can be provided for monetarily outside the mother organisation, but divorced from exercising power/influence in the parent organisational planning and operations. Thus, the interests of the family, employees, investors and the country would be served best.

NUGGETS

- Talent among the young entrants must be spotted early, and their grooming entrusted to gurus (managers).
- Managements/owners must ensure that only the most competent and deserving person is made the head of the organisation.

5. Dronacharya
(The Ancient Story)

1. Hastinapur was the capital of the Kaurava kingdom. One day, the young Kauravas (sons of the blind king Dhritrashtra) and Pandavas (sons of Pandu) were playing on the outskirts of the capital with a ball. The ball accidently fell into a well. The princes were able to see the ball, which was floating on the surface of the water but had no way to get it back. Amidst all the hustle and bustle involved in their efforts and while giving various suggestions to retrieve the ball, the ring worn by Yudhishtra (the eldest of the Pandavas) also fell into the well.

2. Coincidentally, at that point of time, a Brahmin, carrying a bow and arrows, happened to be passing by. On seeing the distress of the princes, he offered to help them out. He assured them that he would retrieve both the ball and the ring. He asked the princes to gather a number of reed sticks. The Brahmin sharpened one end of each reed and left the other round. He shot the first reed into the ball from the well; and by shooting one reed into another made a string of reeds and recovered the ball; later the ring was similarly retrieved.

3. The princes were amazed at the Brahmin's skill and took him to their grandfather Bheeshma Pitamah. Bheeshma was also very impressed by the Brahmin and appointed him the 'guru' for teaching archery and other military techniques to the princes. The Brahmin proved himself to be an expert teacher, imparting both skills and wisdom. He enjoyed full respect from all the princes. He was named Dronacharya (i.e., Drona the guru).

1. Organisations will be confronted with setbacks and accidents in the normal course of operations or while carrying out extracurricular activities, irrespective of the precautions taken and the safety measures instituted. Managers must train their subordinates to be able to take rational decisions under stress conditions: this can best be done through the review of actual events within the organisation and through case studies. Individuals who have special abilities to tackle difficult situations should be identified and delegated the task of handling tricky issues. The manager himself must exercise a high degree of self-control and avoid rushing around aimlessly – the manager's conduct either helps the subordinates to calm down or adds to their panic. If the manager panics, irrational decisions will get taken and the situation will worsen.

2. The effective leader first plans his strategy, secure in his own competence, before initiating any action. Once convinced of the correctness of his approach, he should assign specific tasks to his subordinates commensurate with their abilities. The residual feeling amongst the team on overcoming a difficult situation should be that of increased respect for the leader and that 'we did it'. The hierarchical level should be forgotten during adversity and the most competent manager entrusted with the task of achieving the organisational goals.

3. Every employee in the organisation must be trained to remain alert for identifying talented outsiders whose inclusion in the team would strengthen the organisation. Such alertness becomes much more important in a growing organisation with ambitious plans. Recruiting talented people, at certain points of time, even without clear vacancies, can only prove highly productive in a fiercely competitive globalised market environment. In the employment market there is no dearth of numbers but there is a critical shortage of talented persons.

NUGGETS

- The ability to remain cool in the face of adversity must be developed in all managers.
- Planning skills of managers should be sharpened to tackle   problems logically and successfully.
- Managements must 'grab' suitable talent whenever available and retain and nurture such talent.

6. The Test of Disciples
(The Ancient Story)

1. The Kauravas and the Pandavas were educated at the ashram (residential institution) of Dronacharya, their guru. Each one had been imparted knowledge of many subjects and also physical and manual skills.

2. The period of stay at the ashram and the education course were nearing completion. At that stage, Dronacharya decided to test all his disciples. The idea of testing the individual skills was suggested to Bheeshma (the grandfather of both Kauravas and Pandavas). This idea was approved and various arrangements for conducting the test were made. Dronacharya made a parrot of clay and placed it on the branch of a tree some distance away; the aim of the test was to hit the bird's eye (with a bow and arrow). Bheeshma was himself present among the gathering of various members of the royal court. A large number of other people also collected to witness the outcome of the test.

3. For the test, Dronacharya called the princes forward one by one. Before the individual prince could shoot, Dronacharya questioned him: 'What do you see on the tree?' 'The parrot, the leaves and branches' was generally the reply given to Dronacharya. No one succeeded in hitting the bird's eye. Finally, Arjuna's turn came. When questioned, Arjuna replied: 'Gurudev, I can only see the eye of the parrot.' Saying so, he released the arrow and pierced the bird's eye.

4. All present congratulated Arjuna (a Pandava); but the Kauravas became jealous and unhappy. This was one more reason added to the Kauravas' resolve to seek revenge against the Pandavas at a future date.

1. Each manager is a guru to his subordinates. He must identify the knowledge, values, attitudes and skills that are required by each of the subordinates in order to succeed in achieving the goals, both at present and in the future. This should form the basis for teaching, training and counselling. As a guru, the manager should treat his relationships with his juniors as of long-term value, comparable to the stay in an ashram. This automatically leads to genuine caring and concern for subordinates.

2. Before launching the subordinate into a new job or assignment, it is important to evaluate his capability. Thus, there needs to be a *performance appraisal system*. The top management, like Bheeshma, must be fully involved in the formulation of the performance appraisal policy and must personally oversee its effective implementation. The procedural part can be delegated. Also, the evaluation system must be common to all those at an equal level and related to their knowledge/skill areas. The system must be made well known to all so that they can judge its fairness. The top management must participate in the demonstrated performance evaluation of vitally important members. The aim/goal must be clearly explained by the leader, as far as possible in quantifiable terms, to each person concerned. It is also necessary to check if those being evaluated have understood their task. This means laying down of job descriptions, identifying key result areas, jointly setting personal targets and correlating the performance appraisal system with the agreed targets. At all managerial and supervisory levels, attribute evaluation also becomes essential – the meaning/connotation of each attribute must be explained and the evaluation based on actual conduct/ behaviour duly recorded.

3. At any one particular moment, application of total effort
and concentration is needed to achieve the final goal. Every
goal can be divided into 'must achieve', 'should achieve', and
'could achieve' aspects. Total thrust must go into achieving
the 'must' portion first.

---

4. The success achieved by the talented persons tends to
create jealousies. Top managements should reward the
talented, based on achievements seen and acknowledged by
others. Jealous people float rumours, play down the achievements
of the successful persons and also create hurdles in their
path. The successful ones tend to suffer from the 'euphoria
of success', arrogance and a false sense of indispensability.
Managements must remain alert to such behaviour of both
the jealous and the successful; deviant behaviour must be
stopped as soon as it shows up, in order to avoid having to
confront a major problem in the future.

NUGGETS

- The top management is accountable for an effective
  performance appraisal system.
- Immediate remedial action on observing the first
  signs of deviant behaviour is a must.

7. Arjuna and Subhadra
(The Ancient Story)

1. Arjuna once visited Dwarka to spend a few days with his friend Lord Krishna. There Arjuna met Lord Krishna's cousin (sister) Subhadra and fell in love with her. The custom then prevalent amongst the Kshatriyas (martial races) was to either win the lady-love in an open contest of skills or carry her away by force. Organising a contest of skills was a long drawn-out process; carrying away by force was the quicker answer. However, it often led to war or taking of revenge by the aggrieved party. On a hint from Lord Krishna, Arjuna carried away Subhadra by design. Balrama, the elder brother of Lord Krishna, was furious on hearing of Arjuna's action and wanted to punish him.

2. Knowing that Lord Krishna and Arjuna were very close friends, Balrama decided to call a council meeting before taking any action. In the council meeting, after much debate, Lord Krishna's counsel prevailed. Lord Krishna described the illustrious family background of Arjuna and the possibility of Balrama facing defeat in battle against the invincible Arjuna. Lord Krishna counselled that they should bring back Arjun and Subhadra, with due respect, and get them officially married. This would further strengthen the friendly relations between two powerful families; thus, as allies, they would be much stronger together in facing a hostile world.

1. Some leaders develop special competence in long-term planning. They can conceptualise future events and initiate action according to a very clear design in order to meet forthcoming contingencies. The logic behind such action should be known only to a confined circle, so that the confidentiality of strategic thinking is maintained. Some other senior managers in the organisation may not clearly understand the various ramifications, and may, as result thereof, express their dissent; the dissenters would need to be explained the relevant logic, so as to ensure that willingly or otherwise they do not become obstacles to organisational progress.

2. Meetings provide a useful method of solving difficult problems, through open and objective airing of contradictory views, discussing in detail the various pros and cons of an issue and finally arriving at a course of action by consensus. Such a consensus ties down all participants to common thinking and obtains their commitment as individuals and as a group. Such meetings are fruitful only if the most powerful do not thrust their views down everybody's throat and are prepared to listen patiently with an open mind and finally, abide by a group decision. These meetings should have a specific agenda and must not degenerate into a meaningless exchange of long-winded presentations. Decisions, once taken, must be followed up by appropriate action, duly monitored, if results are to be obtained. Organisational interests are best served by identifying and developing powerful allies whether they be customers, vendors, competitors or authorities (central, state or regional).

NUGGETS

- Managers must ensure confidentiality of long-term strategic organisational plans.
- Team deliberations are fruitful for successfully resolving complex issues and problems.
- Allies are needed to win in a highly competitive business environment.

8. Drona and Drupad
(The Ancient Story)

1. Drona (later titled as Dronacharya) and Drupad were once classmates in the ashram of Sage Agnivesha. Drona was a poor Brahmin and Drupad, the prince from the kingdom of Panchala. Drona and Drupad became fast friends. Drupad promised to share everything with Drona, once he became the king. On completion of their education, they went their own ways. Drupad, in due course, was crowned the king of Panchala. Drona continued to remain poor and faced tremendous difficulty in making a living. Drona's son was continuously ridiculed, because of his poverty, by his classmates. Drona's patience came to an end and he decided to seek the help of his old friend Drupad.

2. Drona, accompanied by his wife and son, reached the court of Drupad. The king refused to even recognise Drona and forgot the promises he had made to his classmate; Drupad also used harsh words to disgrace Drona. Thus were sown the seeds of a life-long enmity.

1. Organisations conduct various training programmes to impart knowledge, skills, values or correct attitudes through heightened self-awareness. The participants in such programmes should be treated as equals by the faculty — the learning process would be hampered if the level of the individual in the organisation were to decide the correctness of the persons' views. Such programmes lead not only to sharing of experiences and knowledge among the participants but also to better understanding and greater acceptance of each other. Intelligently organised residential programmes can lead to building of strong interpersonal relationships; may be not in the group as a whole, but definitely among smaller subgroups. Relationships so built can be easily sustained over long periods of time, through regular communication and meetings. The successful top management will receive requests for help from their 'not-so-fortunate' old associates. Whether to extend help or not becomes a matter of personal attitudes and values. Organisations cannot lay down a rigid policy to handle such requests, since they are made to a specific individual by an old personal associate -- such a decision would be purely a personal decision.

2. Many persons who reach the top rungs of organisations tend to isolate themselves from the lower levels. They use their time to socialise and interact with only those of an equivalent status, as a matter of misplaced arrogance. The worst crime is not to extend recognition to old associates, when they arrive seeking help, as also using harsh words to exhibit one's power and superiority. Top managers, at times, have been known to make people seeking their help wait endlessly and call them repeatedly without extending any help whatsoever. Others in the organisation observe such behaviour and start commenting on the kind of 'concern' that their seniors have for people -- a trend likely to hurt the morale in the long run. Dealing with humility and kindness, while expressing an inability to help, will not convert old associates into enemies and will be more palatable to all concerned.

NUGGETS

- Effectively conducted residential management development programmes help foster and maintain emotional bonds.
- Managers are judged by other employees on the basis of their behaviour.
- Never ridicule others so as to leave behind residual antagonism, just because they are from lower levels, because one never knows when they may be the ones who can give help and assistance.

9. The House of Shellac
(The Ancient Story)

1. Dhritrashtra (a Kaurava) had decided to crown Yudhishtra (a Pandava) as the king. The other Kauravas became furious and jealous; they decided to kill the Pandavas. Duryodhana made secret plans to send the Pandavas to 'Varanavati', where a palace was specially built out of shellac (a combustible material), which was to be torched when the Pandavas were living in it. Dhritrashtra was eventually persuaded by Duryodhana to send the Pandavas on a journey to Varanavati and stay in the special palace. The Pandavas were fully aware of the threat from Kauravas and remained perpetually alert. When they came to know of this diabolical plot, the Pandavas managed to secretly dig an escape tunnel in the special palace of shellac.

2. One day, a Bhil (tribal) woman came along with her five sons, to stay for the night. By coincidence that very night, the Pandavas were also at Varanavati. The Kauravas set the palace ablaze. The Pandavas, at the first smell of smoke, fled through the escape tunnel, but the Bhil woman and her sons died in the fire. The Kauravas mistook the charred bodies of the Bhil family to be those of Kunti and Pandavas; the former were happy, little aware that the Pandavas had, in reality, escaped.

1. Top management decisions must be, as far as possible, free of bias and based on 'what is right' in the best interests of the organisation. Top managers should not get persuaded to change their decisions for the personal gain of an individual/department/group. Managers and leaders have to objectively study the person profile, attributes, attitudes, values and competence of their bosses, peers and subordinates. Thus, they will be in a position to predict the behaviour of others under different conditions. This allows the manager to remain alert to likely dangers. Another role that a manager has to play is that of counselling people; irrespective of their hierarchical level, so as to moderate behaviour for the organisational good. In the absence of effective counselling, undesirable behaviour is engendered and keeps repeating itself. Understanding and accepting objectively the reality of organisational reward to others will tend to reduce manipulation and politicisation. Yet there are vengeful or vicious persons in an organisation; managers should spend greater effort in bringing them on the right track or effect their separation from the organisation. The 'dangerous ones' plot and plan in secrecy and go to great pains to bring about a situation adverse to their peers earmarked for promotion. They are smooth, slimy and smart operators; very often, they hoodwink the simple and naïve persons to conform to their way of thinking and use them as tools to achieve their ends.

2. The wise manager keeps himself ready to face dangers. He identifies the direction, nature and seriousness of the threat facing him. The timing of its occurrence is a matter of guestimate. Situations call for round-the-clock watch-fulness. Contingency plans and escape routes have to be thought out and executed carefully, to make them opera-tional at short notice. In case of organisational conflicts

among the powerful heavyweights, quite often the innocent
suffer. Lower level employees tend to become sacrificial
pawns. The powerful get hurt marginally and manage to
escape by blaming the totally or partially innocent.
Organisations must remain alert to such conflicts and
ensure that the innocent do not suffer.

NUGGETS

- Top managements are accountable for operating
  in the best organisational interest.
- The 'boss' must keep internal conflicts under
  control.

10. Establishing the Pandava Kingdom
(The Ancient Story)

1. King Dhritrashtra summoned his royal council, on the return of the Pandavas from self-imposed exile after their escape from the house of shellac, and a decision was taken to partition the kingdom. The eastern part with its capital at Hastinapur and containing fertile lands was given to the Kauravas; while the western part containing forest land and wilderness went to the Pandavas. Dhritrashtra became the king of the Kauravas and Yudhishtra the king of the Pandavas. The Pandavas toiled hard and built a new capital, Indraprastha (later renamed Delhi). Being righteous, they were blessed by all the gods and Rishis (saints), who had assembled for the coronation of Yudhishtra.

2. On the completion of coronation ceremonies, Lord Krishna wished to return to his own kingdom of Dwarka. Prior to his departure, he highlighted, to Yudhishtra, the fundamental principles for determining a king's conduct. Eternal vigilance is the price a king must pay for the safety of his kingdom and must guard it with care. He must watch over the welfare of his people with a father's love, the strength of a friend and save them from external dangers. He must also ensure the rule of justice, tinged with a human approach. The king must neither discriminate amongst his people nor grant favours to particular persons. With this guidance, Lord Krishna blessed the Pandavas and bid them farewell.

1. The top management should take all critical decisions after due consultations with the immediate subordinates. It is such immediate subordinates who convert decisions into goal-oriented actions; their participation in the formulation of the goals generates their commitment to them both as individuals and as a team. Joint goal-setting results in the various team members extending support and understanding to each other, thus providing a unidirectional thrust. The top management team is also the conscience-keeper of the organisation. Personal prejudices of the top man may, at times, vitiate equitable treatment of the subordinates. Managers must have the courage to voice strong dissent to ensure fair decision-making. In the overall analysis, *ad hoc* and whimsical decisions by the top management adversely affect their credibility in the eyes of the subordinates. Consequently, the talented leave and non-thinkers continue to serve the organisation for lack of opportunities offered by the employment market. Such a situation is highly detrimental to long-term organisational interests. Setting up a new business venture or project calls for intelligence linked to a high degree of hard work, over a long period of time. The value system brought in when the organisation is in its infancy sustains it for a long period. Working together under difficult conditions, happily sharing the meagre resources available, and extending support to each other develops emotional bonds and, above all, the intrinsic qualities, both good and bad, of a person manifest themselves clearly when working under such conditions.

2. The top management's tasks can be classified as (i) control of current operations, (ii) going in for futuristic planning and organising and (iii) staffing for the long term. The futuristic aspects should take away at least 60 per cent of the top management time. This will mean objective evaluation of (i) likely threats, (ii) dynamics of the business environment, (iii) growth/diversification opportunities, (iv) public relations needed at the highest level with all external interfacing agencies and (v) the necessity of establishing links with appropriate allies. The control of current operations would mean setting/manualising/implementing of fair policies; monitoring and helping in achievement of corporate targets; building cohesive, competent, satisfied teams; and creating an organisational climate which is friendly and fair and is guided by organisation policies and the laws of the land.

NUGGETS

- Participative decision-making strengthens the organisation.
- Managers must have the courage to voice dissent.
- The top management must focus both on the current and futuristic aspects – the latter are as, if not more, important.

11. The Pandavas and Sage Vyasa
(The Ancient Story)

1. Yudhishtra, along with the other Pandavas, came to Hastinapur when invited by the Kauravas for a game of dice. The Kshatriyas, as per age-old customs, could not decline such an invitation. After Yudhishtra had lost the game (and all his possessions too), the Pandavas proceeded into exile. The Pandavas lost because Shakuni (the maternal uncle of the Kauravas) was a past master at manipulation, and played with charmed dice, which always turned out as he wanted them to.

2. While the Pandavas were residing in the forest, Sage Vyasa once visited them. He predicted a terrible war between the Pandavas and the Kauravas at the end of the period of the Pandavas' banishment. Sage Vyasa advised the Pandavas to start preparation for the forthcoming war by acquiring divine weapons through prayers/meditation and pleasing the gods. Arjuna was instructed to go to Lord Shiva on Kailash mountain and obtain the most powerful weapons in the world. The Pandavas followed the advice of Sage Vyasa and became equipped with divine weapons, well ahead of the predicted war.

1. In old, well-established organisations there are a large number of customs, traditions and practices which get accepted as norms of behaviour. More often than not, these features are not reduced to the written form but are taken for granted; the older employees set personal examples in following these codes and new entrants are suitably guided by their mentors/bosses. As time passes, these features tend to go out of tune with reality and need to be looked at analytically to update them with the changing social, moral and economic realities. Industries which are located in the hinterland tend to remain more traditional and, therefore, need to be more alert to this danger. The younger generation members, who are drawn from better educational institutions, try to stay away from industries with a very traditional image, since they are afraid of getting 'suffocated'. Such industries need to change their ways and adopt novel methods to attract and retain talent. Some old-time employees survive on manipulation, rather than on their competence. Such individuals need to be watched carefully, both by the management and by other individuals to ensure their own personal safety. These manipulators, because of old associations, wield far more power than they deserve.

2. Wise managements develop the ability to guestimate the future, based on hard work. This means collecting data, establishing trends, breaking away from established thinking, becoming creative and monitoring the validity of the guestimates. In a world becoming increasingly smaller in this age of multifarious forms of rapid communication, this ability has to be developed and nurtured. Then and then alone, would it be possible to prepare for effectively coping with the challenges of the future. Currently effective men, machines, materials and technology tend to gradually lose their effectiveness as time passes, rendering their updating, through training, research and development, absolutely essential. This updating also involves injecting of fresh blood and talented youngsters into the organisation. Unless detailed plans for updating of the various resources are made, meticulously implemented and constantly monitored, an organisation will tend to lose its leadership/goodwill in the market.

NUGGETS

- Past practices must not become a handicap to the organisation.
- Continuous organisational renewal is essential for survival.

12. The Pandavas Seek the Return of Their Kingdom
(The Ancient Story)

1. After the exile period had terminated, Yudhishtra demanded back his kingdom of Indraprastha. Dhritrashtra was willing to return Indraprastha, but his son Duryodhana was adamant in his refusal. Subsequently, in the council hall of King Virata, gathered Lord Krishna, the Pandavas and many other chieftains. Lord Krishna lauded the righteous behaviour of the Pandavas and their having lived by the terms of exile – he emphasised their right to get back Indraprastha so that Yudhishtra could look after his people.

2. During the discussions, differing opinions were expressed. Some suggested patience and others recommended going to war. Drupad, the aged king of Panchala, recommended going to war, because Duryodhana was stubborn and misconstrued the mildness of the Pandavas as their weakness. He also suggested sending ambassadors to other kingdoms to find allies. However, one last effort had to be made to arrive at a peaceful solution. The last mission of the ambassador of the Pandavas (Lord Krishna) to Dhritrashtra failed because of Duryodhana's stubbornness, and the Pandavas decided to declare war on the Kauravas. Dhritrashtra then sent his charioteer Sanjay to persuade Yudhishtra to restrain the Pandavas from use of force to get their rightful share by highlighting the evil dimensions of war. Yudhishtra was not persuaded, since he was convinced that whereas it was good to maintain peace, but not when it meant running away from one's duty. The stage was thus set for the war.

1. All organisations have to interact with other organisations in the course of their business – whether they be represented by customers, suppliers, government authorities, etc. The transactions generally take place on the basis of written documents; however, once faith and credibility have been established between two parties, verbal communication suffices. Organisations which break such contracts, without negotiating terms afresh, develop a bad public image; others become reluctant to deal with such organisations and stop accommodating them. Eventually, such interorganisational differences multiply and lead to severe conflicts and litigation. The voice of sanity raised by the honest few gets overwhelmed by those more powerful and intent on pursuing their own selfish ways. In a managerial capacity, the courage to stand up boldly and confront such situations is an in-built occupational hazard.

2. The good are often misread as being weak. Up to a certain point, goodness must be practised, but, at times, resorting to ruthless action in a competitive market is essential. Unfair practices of other organisations, if hurting you, must be pointed out and negotiations started to settle matters amicably; however, at times, 'tit for tat', even though unpleasant, must be resorted to. It has been observed that sometimes this phenomenon also operates between managements and unions within an organisation. Careful planning must precede initiating of ruthless action; it is necessary to ascertain the correct legal position, find competent and strong allies and know the strengths and weaknesses of the opposing group. The 'wrong-doer' will try and project his actions as being righteous, and tender advice subtly to create differences amongst the members in the competing organisation. Once it is decided to take a tough stand, there should be no withdrawing till the wrong-doer is suitably punished.

NUGGETS

- Managements must never negotiate out of fear but should also not fear to negotiate.
- The business environment demands fairness coupled with firmness.
- At times, in the larger interest of the organisation, it is necessary for a manager to be ruthless and firm in taking decisions.

13. Abhimanyu and the Wheel Formation
(The Ancient Story)

1. During the battle of Kurukshetra, the armies could adopt a particular battle arrangement called the 'Chakravyuha' or 'wheel formation'. This formation needed tremendous knowledge, leadership qualities and skill to organise and, therefore, it lay within the capability of very few persons. On the other hand, equal mastery of skills and the usage of arms was required to break into and out of the Chakravyuha.

2. One particular day, Arjuna started explaining the wheel formation to his pregnant wife, but could only complete the narration of how to break into such an arrangement. Abhimanyu, who was at that time in his mother's womb, acquired this partial knowledge of breaking into the wheel formation, but not how to come out of it. Arjuna was the only Pandava who had the total requisite knowledge. Abhimanyu suffered from this limitation. During the Kurukshetra war, the Kauravas adopted the wheel formation. Arjuna was preoccupied elsewhere on the battlefield and Abhimanyu took it upon himself to defeat the designs of the enemy. Abhimanyu broke into the wheel formation and killed many of the enemy through sheer bravery, but in the end met a hero's death, as he could not break out of the Chakravyuha.

1. Knowledge, as applicable in organisations, is of two varieties: (i) general functional knowledge and (ii) highly advanced specialised knowledge. Managers having the latter are major assets; they contribute to the basic strength and the continued growth of the organisation. Such people are few and difficult to recruit and retain; organisations must absorb such people and ensure they become dedicated, long-serving, competent team members.

2. It is essential for the top-level management to train competent subordinates. In this context, the difficulties arise, because gifted and talented specialists can sometimes be 'egoists', loners, poor teachers and may not possess enough patience and tolerance to understand the genuine natural deficiencies of juniors. Therefore, the selection of subordinates to be trained has to be done carefully and with the total concurrence of the specialists. Continuous challenges need to be posed to the specialists so that they internalise the need for competent subordinates and undertake to develop the latter's abilities and skills. Specialists who become real 'gurus' to their subordinates build up deep emotional bonds with them. It has been seen that if and when such specialists leave the organisation, other than on retirement, their subordinates also follow suit. Consequently, organisations have to develop emotional bonds, both with the specialists and their subordinates, as also understand the motivation patterns of the subordinates to be able to retain them, if the specialist happens to leave. The progress of acquisition of knowledge by the subordinates has to be given direction and monitored in a very delicate manner so as not to upset the specialist. General experience reveals that specialists are callous towards formalised documentation; do not adhere to normal codes of dress and timings; get irritated by elaborate procedures for the acquisition of

resources; and tend to possess their own eccentricities. Organisations must keep all these factors in view and deal with such specialists accordingly.

NUGGETS

- Individuals with highly specialised knowledge and/or skills are organisational assets.
- Innovative specialists who contribute substantially to organisational growth need to be handled differently.

14. Duryodhana in Grief
(The Ancient Story)

1. Abhimanyu, the son of Arjuna, had broken into the *Chakravyuha* (wheel formation) of the Kaurava army and was wreaking havoc killing many soldiers. Lakshmana, seeing his father Duryodhana deeply perturbed by this battlefield disaster, decided to fight Abhimanyu. Lakshmana was no match for Abhimanyu and died fighting. Duryodhana, on hearing of his son's death, was not only heart-broken but also mad with anger. He instructed his warriors to disobey the ethical codes of war to avenge the death of Lakshmana.

2. Abhimanyu was surrounded by several great warriors and attacked from the rear, an unacceptable action in war, which resulted in his death. The violation of this war code opened the way for retaliation from the Pandavas. In the final battle, under guidance from Lord Krishna, Bheema attacked Duryodhana and broke his thigh-bone before killing him, which was also in violation of the war code. However, this act was justified as 'tit for tat'.

1. In family-managed organisations, generally, the younger generation members are placed in positions of power and responsibility which are not commensurate with their maturity. Exposure to higher levels of technical expertise and management knowledge helps in developing conceptual abilities. The theoretical principles learnt call for effective application in a dynamic but hostile business environment, in order to obtain the required results. Profitable application demands maturity with regard to: (i) a technique known as *SWOT* (strengths, weaknesses, opportunities and threats) *analysis* of the organisation/teams/individuals; (ii) knitting teams together; (iii) the ability to work with diverse people; and (iv) coping with changing market demands. It is important that the young generation family members be properly groomed and delegated powers in a graduated manner. Use of excess power by an immature mind can result in either disproportionate success or failure; both situations are not fruitful. Such success would give a distorted sense of self-worth, whereas such failure would cause frustration and a tendency to blame others, rather than trying to understand and overcome one's own shortcomings.

2. In moments of acute organisational adversity, top management must not take hasty decisions. Normally, decisions taken under a state of severe emotional disturbance or stress will invariably be irrational, and could prove dangerous in the long term. At such moments, the entire team should come together and thrash out the vexatious issues. The dissenting arguments should be carefully weighed and reviewed. The work culture should facilitate open expression, rather than suppress dissent. There are two sides to every coin – the top man, as normally happens, callously brushes aside those with differing views. Such high-handedness hurts organisational interest. Embarking on an unhealthy practice opens the doors for others to do the same – be they partners, customers, suppliers, competitors or union leaders. Therefore, laying down of value/policy guidelines and adhering to them would prove the best for the long-term interests of the organisation.

NUGGETS

- Younger family members brought into the family business must be given responsibility commensurate with their competence.
- Such younger members must be initiated at the grassroots level so that they get to know the basic operations and activities essential for taking critical decisions subsequently.
- Initiating unhealthy practices makes organisations vulnerable to a similar backlash.

Part III

Ramayana

15. Valya Koli (Valmiki)
(The Ancient Story)

1. Valya Koli was a dacoit who lived in a forest. He looted innocent travellers who passed through the forest. Sage Narad once happened to be travelling through this forest. Valya Koli confronted Sage Narad and threatened to kill him unless he parted with all his valuables. Sage Narad explained to Valya Koli that the latter was committing a sin by killing and robbing innocent travellers. Valya Koli explained that this was his method of providing for his family. On Sage Narad's suggestion, Valya Koli went to his family and asked them that since they enjoyed the fruits of his acts, would they also share his sins? The family members refused to do so and bluntly told him that it was his job to provide for the family; how he did so was his responsibility.

2. Valya Koli was shocked and decided to change his ways. When he approached Sage Narad for help, the latter advised him to chant the name of Lord Rama, whereby all his sins would be washed away. For several years Valya performed a penance, constantly, chanting 'Rama, Rama'. Because of the divinity of Lord Rama's name, all his sins were forgiven, and Valya Koli, the cruel dacoit, became Sage Valmiki, the author of Ramayana.

1. Every manager has to understand and accept the fact that he alone is accountable for all actions, good or bad, initiated by him. In trying to achieve his objectives, the means adopted are as important as the results. Wrong means will fetch him rewards in the short run, but he will suffer in the long run. The subordinates will enjoy the benefits of the results achieved, but will disclaim any responsibility when caught in any wrong-doing by stating that their actions were performed only to carry out the orders given by the manager. It often happens that when managers are caught for doing the wrong things, their subordinates desert them or turn informants against them. This also shows that no manager can keep all his subordinates happy all the time; the disgruntled or unhappy ones tend to, become informants. Managers must, therefore, when using unethical means, be fully aware of the risk they are taking. Alert managers, when counselled or advised by their subordinates/consultants/outsiders, evaluate the advice given carefully. They check the credibility and correctness of the advice, by brainstorming or discussing with the subordinates. The views of the subordinates are listened to attentively. Subsequently, the manager must evaluate the various views, by himself. Deciding on the future course of action is, again, the manager's sole responsibility.

2. Wise and capable managers, having once decided on a course of action, work very hard, sincerely and to the best of their ability, to achieve the desired results. Dedicated and intelligent efforts pay off in the long run and managements are usually generous enough to forgive past mistakes.

NUGGETS

- Ultimate accountability always remains with the manager.
- Dedicated and intelligent hard work is the sure way to success.

16. The Valour of Rama and Lakshmana
(The Ancient Story)

1. The four brothers Rama, Lakshmana, Bharata, and Shatrughna were taught the Vedas and the skills of archery by Sage Vasishtha. The brothers loved and admired each other deeply. Rama was regarded as the 'lord', by the other three. One day, Sage Vishwamitra visited their father, King Dasharatha (of Ayodhya) and requested that Rama and Lakshmana accompany him. They were required to drive away the demons who continuously disturbed the rishis during the prayer ceremonies. King Dasharatha was worried about the safety of Rama and Lakshmana; but Sage Vasishtha intervened and reassured King Dasharatha, and both the brothers were permitted to go with Sage Vishwamitra.

2. While travelling along the banks of the River Sarayu, Sage Vishwamitra, Rama and Lakshmana entered a dense forest. There, they were attacked by a fearsome she-demon called Tratika. Under Sage Vishwamitra's instructions, Lord Rama fought and killed Tratika. Sage Vishwamitra was very pleased. Lord Rama and Lakshmana later reached the ashram of Sage Vishwamitra. There the prayer ceremonies (*yagnas*) started and, soon, several demons came to disturb the proceedings. Lord Rama and Lakshmana killed many demons and provided safety for the performance of *yagnas* without any disturbance.

1. In an organisation or a group, it is important for its members to develop emotional bonds. Such bonds are developed through sharing of common goals, values, attitudes, successes and adversities. The leaders in an organisation are normally promoted from within, but at times, they can be recruited from outside. The management needs to be very careful in appointing leaders. At times the groups themselves throw up their leaders – this often happens in groups of peers, e.g., workers. This phenomenon also repeats itself in committees, project teams and the like, where the best automatically show up and become *de-facto* group leaders. In departments where subordinates show promising talent, the boss should encourage them to take up a leadership role, rather than threaten them and keep them down.

2. The elders tend to be cautious by nature and, in a genuine way, are concerned about the safety of the younger people. The former groom the latter and want to expose them (the younger persons) gradually to facing the realities of the world on their own. This is a common phenomenon in industry. The talented persons, when caught up in a difficult situation, are able to perform excellently and all their hidden qualities/potential come to the surface. Over-sheltering of talent is good neither for the organisation nor for the individual; the talented ones learn from their mistakes, internalise their failures and develop winning strategies for the future. The talented gain the respect of others by demonstrating excellent levels of performance.

NUGGETS

- The talented persons, when held accountable, perform excellently.
- Such persons automatically become leaders in a group situation.

---

17. Sita Swayamvar
(The Ancient Story)

1. During the course of his travels, King Janak of Mithila once found a beautiful baby girl in a field. He brought her up as his own daughter, and named her 'Sita'. King Janak had a bow of Lord Shiva; it was very heavy and many strong men were required to move it. However, Sita could easily lift it and play with it. This phenomenon amazed King Janak. Sita grew into a beautiful young woman and King Janak decided to organise a 'test of skills' to choose a suitable husband for her. He proclaimed that whoever lifts and strings Shiva's bow would win Sita's hand in marriage.

2. Sage Vishwamitra came to know about the competition, and brought Lord Rama and Lakshmana to Mithila. Many kings from distant lands also came for the *Swayamvar*. At the sight of the huge bow of Lord Shiva, many of them hesitated even to try to lift it. The king of Lanka, Ravana, entered arrogantly and tried to lift the bow, but failed. A number of people present observed Ravana's behaviour and jeered at his failure. Sage Vishwamitra then asked Lord Rama to go ahead. Rama bowed his head in respect, and was able to easily lift the bow. As he was about to string the bow, it broke with a cracking sound. Rama had won the contest; Sita placed the garland around his neck. Lord Rama and Sita were married and everyone rejoiced. However, Ravana, the king of Lanka, felt jealous and humiliated and vowed to take revenge.

1. In the young new entrants who join industry, talent shows itself in work as well as in extracurricular activities. The top management should interact with the young entrants and help in spotting the talented ones. Between senior 'line' and 'staff' managers (particularly those in the older age group) and the young entrants, a generation gap exists. This gap leads to the creation of barriers and more so if senior managers happen to be frustrated. Such barriers are not conducive to growth, and, in such cases, young talented entrants leave the organisation. Pressures of work, hardened attitudes and the value systems of the seniors also reduce their ability to develop healthy interpersonal relationships with the younger generation. Performance evaluation must be undertaken to select the best. The system must have the attributes of: (i) being open; (ii) leading to setting of clear goals; (iii) each individual getting a fair opportunity; (iv) results being made visible based on objectively demonstrated performance; and (v) linking rewards to goal achievement.

2. It is important that every manager carry out self-evaluation. Also, the evaluation of a task and its demands on time, energy and effort must be done. A realistic assessment of a person's strengths and weaknesses and task requirements will enable that person to openly and clearly realise his potential and abilities and not undertake tasks beyond his capabilities. Taking on tasks beyond a person's capability leads to failure and loss of credibility in the eyes of others in the organisation. Arrogance is a pitfall. Competence coupled with humility earns respect from even an enemy or a detractor in the organisation. The arrogant are disliked by all within the organisation as also the external public. This trait makes one lose friends and well-wishers, and non-receipt of feedback on areas needing improvement blocks self-development. The achievement of goals should be made visible to all peers and seniors in the organisation. Rewards thus granted are generally viewed as fair; they motivate others to attain higher levels of performance and establish the credibility of the management. There are many disgruntled persons who will be jealous, will like to play down the achievement of others and may constantly remain on the lookout for opportunities to play the game of 'one-upmanship'. The management and the successful managers should remain alert to such dangers.

NUGGETS

- Spotting of young talent and its proper grooming become the top management's responsibility.
- The reward system must be fair, open and, as far as possible, quantitative data-based.
- Healthy competition must be encouraged within an organisation.

18. The Exile of Rama
(The Ancient Story)

1. King Dasharatha was growing old and therefore, decided to hand over his kingdom to his eldest son – Rama. Rama was loved and respected by all for his good deeds, qualities and temperament. The news was met with joy, and preparations were undertaken for the succession. King Dasharatha had three wives. Queen Kaikeyi, the third and the youngest wife, had a wicked person as her maid, Manthra. Kaikeyi's mind was poisoned by Manthra and she decided that her son Bharata should supersede Rama and become the king.

2. Kaikeyi went into a sulk. When King Dasharatha wanted to know the reason for her anger, Kaikeyi emotionally blackmailed King Dasharatha and forced him to grant the two unconditional boons he had promised her in the past. First, she wanted Bharata to be crowned 'king' and, secondly, Rama sent into exile for fourteen years. King Dasharatha was deeply shocked and distressed by these demands. However, finally Lord Rama himself convinced Dasharatha that it was his (Rama's) moral duty to honour the promises made by Dasharatha. Lord Rama decided to go into exile; his wife Sita and brother Lakshmana insisted on accompanying him.

3. Bharata, who had been away at his grandparents' place, returned later. He was shocked at the turn of events. Bharata was not desirous of ascending the throne. He made all possible efforts to persuade Lord Rama to come back. Lord Rama convinced Bharata that his duty lay in honouring his late father's promise, and that he himself would return to Ayodhya only after completing fourteen years in exile. Bharat requested for and got Lord Rama's slippers. He then placed them on the throne and ruled Ayodhya in the name of Lord Rama.

1. The top man/owner/entrepreneur/departmental heads have to retire some day. Management succession needs careful planning and must be done well in advance. The individual (successor) should be selected on the basis of his merits, qualities and capabilities, displayed over a fairly long period of time. The succession should take place when the handing over can be done as a planned activity and not as a matter of last-minute rush. The outgoing incumbent can then be used as an 'elder statesman' or a 'sounding board', should the successor consider it necessary. The outgoing individual should not interfere in the organisation's activities, once having retired from it. Followers develop respect and affection for leaders who demonstrate desirable qualities in their style of functioning, conduct and behaviour. The subordinates are the first ones to carry out an objective evaluation of the leader; therefore, the leader must lead by personal example. Influential subordinates, for their own selfish reasons, sometimes tender wrong advice to leaders, which can poison the organisational climate. Leaders must not be guided solely by the advice given — they must objectively evaluate the data, ascertain its pros and cons, correlate it to past policies/practices and only then take a decision. Nominating a clear 'number two' to a leader is a must. This has to be a conscious activity and the decision should be publicly announced. An ambiguous state of affairs leads to unwanted politics and undercutting of one person by another.

2. No leader should make any unconditional promise which has to be honoured in the future. To illustrate this point, let us assume that there is a person with an excellent past record. Is there a guarantee that he will continue to achieve increasingly better results in the future? The business or work environment is bound to change. In such a situation, where is the guarantee that the same person will be able to operate as effectively in the changed conditions? Consequently, promising any person a very bright career could be dangerous. Any unconditional promise can force the top management, through emotional blackmail, to take wrong decisions at a future point of time. This can be adverse to the interests of both the top man and the organisation. Ethical dilemmas are faced, often, in decision-making. In such a predicament, the value system, policies and old practices of the organisation should be used as guidelines for decision-making. At times, it may be judicious to sacrifice a personal commitment made in the larger organisational interest. Developing a clear organisational philosophy and helping all employees to imbibe it help in suitable decision-making at different hierarchical levels.

---

3. The genuinely sagacious and hard-working people engender loyalty. Their supporters stay loyal to them even in difficult situations. In the absence of the manager, they continue to work loyally in the best interests of the organisation. Delegation of total accountability and responsibility by the top man is a delicate matter. The temporary incumbent should be chosen with great care, as much for his capabilities, as for his value system. Emotional bonds of great strength need to be generated, so that they can withstand the assaults of temptation, greed and selfishness.

NUGGETS

- Succession planning needs careful selection and deep thought.
- Leaders engender loyalty by what they *do*, rather than by what they *say*.
- Competent and loyal subordinates need to be kept close to heart.
- Career opportunities should be provided without guarantees. Ascending the ladder of success depends upon one's competence and performance and not on past promises.

19. The Lakshman Rekha
(The Ancient Story)

1. Lord Rama had been banished from the kingdom by his father. He, along with his wife Sita and brother Lakshmana, travelled towards southern India, which was an alien environment for them. During their journey they found many devotees and friends and also encountered a large number of powerful enemies.

2. Ravana, the *danav* (demon) king, having been enamoured of Sita decided to abduct her. He arranged for a 'golden deer' (a demon in disguise) to appear in the vicinity of the *kutia* (hut) where Lord Rama was living in the jungle. Sita saw the 'golden deer' and, wanting it, prevailed upon Lord Rama to capture it. Before leaving, Lord Rama delegated the safety of Sita to Lakshmana and told him not to leave her alone till he returned. Lord Rama went in chase of the 'golden deer'. After a while, Sita heard a voice as if Lord Rama was calling Lakshmana for help – in fact, it was a trick played by the demon (in the form of the 'golden deer') by imitating the voice of Lord Rama. Under extreme pressure from Sita, Lakshmana was forced to leave the *kutia*, thus disobeying the instructions of Lord Rama. Lakshmana, before leaving the premises, however, drew a line (*Rekha*) around the *kutia* and counselled Sita not to cross the line; the line had been endowed with power to destroy anyone who tried to cross it. This became known as the 'Lakshman *Rekha*'.

3. Ravana had spent several years in prayers and obtained divine boons, endowing him with great power. He was also a warrior king known for his bravery and valour. Ravana, despite all his powers, tried but failed to cross the 'Lakshman

(Cont'd. on p. 76)

1. Managers operate in a competitive environment, where both friends and enemies exist. In the present global business context, the situation has become worse because competition has become more fierce. Competitors, both domestic and foreign, are continuously on the lookout to take away what the large profitable organisations have and control their assets for their own selfish interests. Therefore, the managements need to remain constantly alert to fight competition and attract and retain partners in business – be they suppliers, customers, employees, government or the society at large and should not allow success to lead to any slackening in the research and development (R & D) thrust.

2. Effective leaders are those who have a very strict code of conduct, irrespective of the conditions around them. Being in charge of the group, the leader/manager must hold himself accountable for the safety and well-being of his group and also for meeting the needs of the group members. Similarly, the top management should create an organisational culture where every in charge holds himself accountable for his group; is sensitive to dangers of the lure and blandishments offered by unscrupulous persons; delegates tasks to be carried out in his absence; gives instructions which are clear and unambiguous and understood by his subordinates. All those in charge, in the absence of their senior's, must take on additional responsibilities and make full arrangements for the organisation to continue to perform effectively. The seniors have a broader view and greater information at their disposal; consequently, disobeying the seniors' instruction, albeit with the best of intentions, can cause disasters.

(Cont'd. on p. 77)

Rekha'. Ravana then disguised himself as a religious priest and persuaded Sita to cross the Lakshman *Rekha* to give him alms, and was thus able to abduct her. Ravana tricked Sita to cross the 'Lakshman *Rekha*' by generating a false sense of duty in her. Crossing of the 'Lakshman *Rekha*' by Sita, under a delusion, was the beginning of a very difficult period for Lord Rama; it was a prelude to a war between the forces of Lord Rama (representing *Dharma*) and the *danav* forces of Ravana (representing *Adharma*).

3. The ability to withstand emotional manipulation and pressures must be developed to enable one to take logical decisions. Managements must train their people in the science/art of decision-making. A perpetually hostile business environment exists, and both managers and employees must be educated as to the nature of lurking dangers and the best methods to cope with them.

GENERAL OBSERVATIONS

1. Companies need to clearly delineate the 'Lakshman *Rekha*', i.e., demarcate between top management and the management group and unionised employees. The companies should also build up an ethos of self-discipline.

TOP MANAGEMENT AND THE MANAGERIAL GROUP

2. The 'Lakshman *Rekha*' which should be drawn between the top management and the managerial group should be based on the following:

(a) The philosophy or belief or culture, which the top management wishes to use as its guiding light, needs to be known. Decision-making by managers at various levels can reflect organisation-wide commonality only if the broad guidelines are spelt out, understood, practised and monitored regularly.

(b) A pertinent question, at this stage, is: should the management try to regulate managerial behaviour only on the basis of precedence or otherwise? Whereas managers are expected to regulate the behaviour of others, who is to regulate managerial behaviour? This factor is not given due weightage, because of the management's ability to 'hire and fire'. A code of conduct must be evolved, practised and monitored, and also updated, whenever the need arises.

(c) It should be ensured that an accurate, updated organisation chart exists, which should be circulated. The decision-making process should be such that it does not 'short-circuit' the principle of 'unity of command'.

(d) The management should lay down generic expectations from each job, in terms of a *job description* and the identification of *key result areas*. A *personal target-setting system* should operate, which should take into account areas for improving performance, in the light of the dynamic business environment.

(e) The management should formulate and manualise *functional policies* and departmental procedures for cohesive working. These policies will reduce manipulation and facilitate working within known parameters.

(f) The management should, again, formulate and manualise personnel policies on factors such as grades, increments, perquisites, statutory benefits, designations, promotions, performance appraisal/counselling, reward and punishment systems, and management development/training/education. These factors will lay down the terms and conditions of service, leading to automatic reduction of manipulation.

(g) Authority quantums must be laid down in order to facilitate decision-making at appropriate levels and ensure that everybody is clear as to the level at which any specific problem will be resolved.

(h) All policies/systems must be updated at periodic intervals to meet the dynamics of business.

MANAGEMENT-UNION RELATIONS

3. The formulation of the company policy is the prerogative of the top management. For such a policy to become meaningful, it should be implemented in both letter and spirit, thus regulating the behaviour of both the top management and the unionised employees. Such a *'Rekha'* would greatly facilitate the development of harmonious and productive human relations. Over 90 per cent of industrial disputes arise because both parties want to twist a situation to their selfish advantage, without having an appreciation of long-term organisational interests. So very often it has been seen that the managements themselves are not keen to lay down a 'Lakshman *Rekha'*. Even if they do so, they keep flouting it at their convenience in order to make a 'fast buck', thus killing management credibility in the eyes of the unionised employees. It is unrealistic to expect that the unions will take the initiative in these matters.

4. Some of the aspects with regard to which a 'Lakshman *Rekha'* could be drawn by the top management in the case of unionised employees are as follows:

(a) Treating unionised employees as partners in business, in the belief that they also have the larger interests of the organisation at heart. Consequently, developing a system for periodic sharing of information pertaining to future business opportunities, threats, problem areas, organisational performance and concerns/anxieties of the management is necessary. This system will go a long way to soften militancy in the union stance, since the employees will know the truth, rather than live in a world of make-believe based on half-truths.

(b) Reaching an understanding on a fair and equitable method of sharing the prosperity generated. Subsequently, both sides should insist on its being honoured.

(c) Providing and insisting on the use of forums for settling of disputes through negotiations and discussions.

(d) Clearly stipulating a code of discipline and being strong and ruthless in dealing with indiscipline and giving the unambiguous message that the management would prefer to 'close shop', rather than accept the growth of the cancer of indiscipline.

(e) Not allowing the erosion of the basic right of the management to manage; however, to be fair, being open to suggestions and recommendations.

(f) Clearly and repeatedly stating that the management 'will not fear to negotiate but will never negotiate out of fear'.

(g) Imposing self-discipline (for managements) such that none of their actions and decisions hurts the management credibility. (It may feel painful for the moment to do so, but it is beneficial in the long run.)

SELF-DISCIPLINE AND RESTRAINT

5. Up to this point, the concept of 'Lakshman *Rekha*' has been applied to group behaviour only; this concept is equally applicable to individual behaviour too. Occasional deviations from the 'narrow and straight path' of behaviour may be accepted or pardoned at lower levels; however, such leeway is reduced in direct proportion to the rising level of the individual in an organisation. Consequently, the absolute necessity for self-discipline and restraint has to be impressed upon each member of the managerial community as the only acceptable norm of behaviour. A code of conduct must be stipulated, disseminated and adherence to it made mandatory. Ruthless and speedy action against members of the management community for lapses has to be taken and the logic shared with others for a salutary effect.

NUGGETS

- Organisations must clearly stipulate performance expectations from the subordinates.
- A code of conduct must be jointly devised and honoured in all transactions.

20. Lord Rama at the Seashore
(The Ancient Story)

1. During his search for Sita (who had been abducted by Ravana), Lord Rama reached the seashore. Preparations were started to arrange for Lord Rama and his army to cross over to Lanka. Nala and Neela possessed unmatched competence in building bridges. However, the building of such a long bridge across the sea without intermediate supports was not practical. Lord Rama prayed for three days and three nights to the sea god for help, but received no response. In the absence of a positive response, Lord Rama decided to punish the sea god. To Lord Rama the sea god appeared to be haughty and had mistaken Lord Rama's gentleness and desire for peace as a weakness. When threatened the sea god appeared and promised to provide support to the bridge to be built by Nala and Neela.

2. When all was ready for the crossing, Lord Rama prayed to Lord Shiva for his blessings so that he could defeat Ravana and come back victorious. To test Lord Rama, Lord Shiva created a thousand lotus flowers. Lord Rama was enjoined to continue praying and then, when pleased, Lord Shiva would appear and pick up one of the lotus flowers to see if his image was replicated therein. Lord Rama continued to pray. Lord Shiva appeared later and, on finding his image replicated in all the thousand lotus flowers, promised Lord Rama total victory.

1. Managements need to identify the expertise required to be built within the organisation for achieving success. Such an activity must be participative in nature, since, in the final analysis, the managers will be required to train, nurture, test and perfect the desired abilities/skills. Specific plans for individuals and groups should be developed; the inputs should be predetermined and correlated to time schedules for development. Generally, the soft-spoken and helpful managers are at times labelled as lacking in assertiveness and drive. They could be like the iron fist in a velvet glove— their tolerance of ambiguity and manipulative practices is high. However, they do not lack in courage or guts and turn ruthless when pushed into a corner. Therefore, an objective assessment of their strengths needs to be done and superficial judgements should be avoided.

2. The top management needs to continuously test the second level of managers. A human being is consistently subjected to stresses and temptations in several areas such as the work place, family get-togethers and social gatherings. Therefore, subtle changes in individual needs, values, and attitudes keep taking place and, unless correctly evaluated, the organisation may be suddenly faced with deviant behaviour, oft repeated, from managers possessing a good past record. Drastic action can be avoided against such managers, provided the top management is alert and firmly checks deviant behaviour at its very first manifestation. The quantitative and qualitative dimensions of the expected performance must be clearly spelt out to leave no room for ambiguity or subsequent *adhocism* in appraisals. On finding the demonstrated performance to be of the highest level, the top management must unashamedly discriminate in favour of such performers.

NUGGETS

- A manager's sophisticated civil behaviour must not be interpreted as a sign of weakness.
- The management's expectations must be spelt out in quantitative and qualitative terms.
- High performers should be given substantially more rewards than others.

21. Vibheeshan
(The Ancient Story)

1. Ravana was a great devotee of Lord Shiva. Ravana undertook years of rigorous meditation and prayer; finally Lord Shiva was pleased and granted him a boon; which made him almost invincible. Ravana was given a pot of 'divine nectar' (*amrit*), which was placed below his navel. Only when this pot was broken would Ravana be killed. Ravana became arrogant and started committing evil deeds.

2. Vibheeshan, Ravana's brother, was god-fearing and upright who tendered righteous advice to his brother. Vibheeshan voiced his dissent when Ravana returned with the abducted Sita. As Lord Rama was preparing to invade Lanka, Vibheeshan advised Ravana to respectfully return Sita to Lord Rama and negotiate peace. Ravana got very angry and kicked Vibheeshan in the presence of many, in the royal court. Vibheeshan, out of frustration, left Lanka and joined forces with Lord Rama.

3. Lord Rama and Ravana came face to face in the final battle. Despite Lord Rama's best efforts, Ravana still stood strong and continued battling. Finally, Vibheeshan disclosed Ravana's secret of invincibility to Lord Rama, which resulted in the death of Ravana.

1. The relative competence of leaders in any organisation differs substantially. Some leaders achieve miracles through continuous self-development, acquisition and application of knowledge, achievement orientation and goal-directed behaviour. For some others, success engenders an inflated and false sense of self-worth; a tendency to rate others below their real competence; and exaggerated self-righteousness. It also brings power. Power corrupts but absolute power corrupts absolutely. Arrogance, vanity and pride are very often the side-effects of power. Proud people tend to isolate themselves from team members and have a tendency to overpunish others for minor breaches of accepted norms of behaviour. Such leaders, need counselling. If such a leader happens to be the top person, the immediate team members have to bring sanity to decision-making, even at the cost of sacrificing their personal interests for the larger good of the organisation. Irrespective of what one thinks, there is no perfect human being; we all have weak areas and enemies will mercilessly exploit them, as and when the opportunity arises.

2. Power-drunk leaders consider themselves invincible. They deride balanced and mature advice. Ideas and people reflecting their personal views find favour; dissent is punished. Any punishment to a senior manager must be meted out in private and not in front of a gathering, especially of subordinates, as this causes deeper and long-lasting frustration, generating a sense of vengeance. Such behaviour is against the organisational interests. Further, managers at different levels handle information and data of a confidential nature, which, if revealed to outsiders, would damage organisational interests. Turnover in managerial categories is a way of life; it must be accepted by the top management. To lessen the negative impact of separations, the work ethos should build emotional/loyalty bonds, so that even those who leave will not want to harm their old organisation. Also, every organisation needs to carefully analyse as to what is really confidential and what is not, and for what time period. Excessive concern with confidentiality will raise barriers to essential communication and departments/individuals will start operating in isolation, thus greatly hampering the unidirectional thrust of the organisation.

3. Ill-treatment of managers, particularly the very senior and responsible ones, is dangerous. They are in a position to harm their last organisation seriously, if they find allies in competitors. Managers and organisations are not bonded for life; however, the parting can be made fair, humane and without rancour. The talented persons who have shouldered enormous responsibilities should be given a suitable farewell so that they take away a feeling of residual loyalty to the organisation.

NUGGETS

- The management must provide adequate security to critical and confidential information.
- Separations should be handled such that relationships continue in the future.

22. Ram Rajya
(The Ancient Story)

1. After defeating (and slaying) Ravana, Lord Rama returned to Ayodhya (along with Sita and Lakshmana) after his fourteen years in exile, having re-established the rule of the just in Lanka. He was welcomed wholeheartedly by Bharata and the populace. Rama ascended the throne and Bharata served him loyally for long years.

2. In Ram Rajya, prosperity was abounding and was shared by all. Grain harvests, food, fruits, milk and honey were found in abundance. The governance of the kingdom was just, fair and open. The king was accessible and sensitive to the needs of his people. Law and order prevailed. Many years later, a small group of people started talking against Sita, casting doubts about her sanctity and purity, because of her having lived in Ravana's captivity for so long. Lord Rama sent Sita away, despite tremendous personal sorrow, to the ashram of Valmiki.

1. The rightful owners of enterprises and industrial organisations, at times, return after long periods of stay outside the country or after convalescing. Those responsible for management, in the interim period, should consider it their moral duty to hand over the reins to the legal claimants. Moral uprightness would also suggest that the interim incumbents revert to their new role happily and serve the organisation loyally. 'I'-motivated or selfish interim incumbents have, at times, created major obstacles to the re-entry of the rightful owners. Therefore, the appropriate selection of interim management cadres poses very difficult choices. In the present-day world, continued contact and periodic interaction between the legal and interim incumbents becomes an inescapable necessity; the task can be delegated but abdication will be disastrous.

2. Well-managed, growth-oriented organisations generate prosperity. Their success does not stem only from manufacturing good products in increasing numbers but also from fair policies, intelligent hard work, maintaining high moral ethos, sharing of prosperity and progressive people's policies. However, managements must bear in mind the old saying: 'It is not possible to keep 100 per cent of the people pleased 100 per cent of the time.' Managements must remain alert to such disgruntled people and initiate appropriate action. The cause for unhappiness should be quickly understood and remedial measures taken — any delay in taking action always results in the unhappiness spreading like a cancer.

NUGGETS

- Owners may delegate, but never abdicate.
- Discontent, if left unchecked, could be cancerous for the organisation.

Hinduism

23. The Naming of Ganesha
(The Ancient Story)

1. Lord Shiva and his wife Parvati lived on Kailash mountain. At times Shiva would go away for several months to perform penance. During such periods, Parvati had to stay alone. Once Parvati was alone at home and wanted to take a bath. She wondered who would look after the house while she was bathing. Then she had an idea: she removed the sandal paste from her body and moulded it into the form of a boy – her son. She posted her son at the door and told him not to let anyone in until she had finished her bath. The son stood guarding the door; he stopped everyone who came to the house.

2. When Shiva returned home, he was also stopped. The boy guarding the door told Shiva: 'You can't go in, since my mother is having her bath and she has told me not to let anyone in!' Shiva become annoyed, and lost his temper. He chopped off the boy's head with his *trishul* (trident). Parvati, who, on coming out, saw the headless body, started weeping, and uttered: 'Oh my lord! What have you done? You have killed my son!'

3. Shiva felt sorry that he had lost his temper. When Shiva wanted to give back life to the boy, it was found that the head had disappeared. He searched in vain. Shiva sent his servants – called *ganas* – to the jungle and asked them to get the head of the first live being that they could find. The *ganas* came across a lone elephant, cut off its head, and brought it to Shiva. Shiva put the elephant head on the boy's headless body, gave him life and thus made Parvati happy. Since *ganas* had helped to bring the son to life, the boy was named 'Ganesha'.

1. The security of organisational assets has to be carefully planned and organised. Given loose control, temptations arise and losses can take place through thefts and pilferage. The employees tend to become careless in accounting and in using of company property, since no positive or tangible benefits can be expected from the 'boss', for displaying concern and taking action to safeguard company assets. A system for strict monitoring should be established and individuals made specifically accountable. Instructions regarding the management's expectations need to be spelt out in clear and simple terms so that people do not have any lingering doubts regarding their specific roles.

2. The persons who guard company assets tend to become unpopular, more so in the case of senior level managers who dislike being checked or even questioned. Organisational policies should be made clear to them and must be ruthlessly implemented as far as security is concerned. The principle behind such measures is that it is not a question of distrust in the employees but a necessary audit function. All employees are subject to law; rules as formulated, if allowed to be bent, will lead to chaos. The guardians must have the top management's assurance that any complaints arising out of the discharge of their duty will not be entertained. Nevertheless, the guardians *do* need to be courteous at all times. At times human beings will err on the wrong side of the law because of work pressures, or irritability at delays or ego problems. The top management will need to handle such problems delicately, adopting the policy of *'what* is right' and *not 'who* is right' as their guideline.

3. Sometimes, loss of critical or 'A'-class (top security) items can take place. Their recovery can never be certain and, therefore, greater care needs to be exercised for guarding such assets. At times, identical replacements may not be available. The subordinates must be given clear specifications of what is required in terms of quantitative and qualitative parameters; otherwise, the substitute may not really be able to fulfil the precise need, as done by the original.

NUGGETS

- Valuable company assets must be zealously guarded and individual accountability clearly specified.
- Senior managers must display respect for law by personal example.

24. Ganesha and Kartikeya
(The Ancient Story)

1. Ganesha had a younger brother named Kartikeya. Ganesha was clever and sweet natured while Kartikeya was short-tempered. Sometimes, while playing, they quarrelled. Once they were involved in a serious altercation and went to their parents to decide who was at fault.

2. To settle the disagreement Shiva suggested that they both go around the world; the one who came first would be considered right.

3. Kartikeya rode a peacock, while Ganesha's means of transport was a little rat. Kartikeya was confident that he would win since his peacock was much faster than the rat. Ganesha knew that he could never win the race outright. Therefore, Ganesha had a bright idea. He made his mother and father stand together and quickly went around them three times.

4. On returning, Kartikeya claimed that he had won. Ganesha said firmly that since Shiva and Parvati were the world, going around them was like going around the world, which he had done thrice, and hence he was the winner.

5. Ganesha was declared the winner by Parvati. Kartikeya lost his temper, thinking that Parvati was being partial to Ganesha.

1. All humans have their individual strengths and weaknesses. In the organisational context, the *performance appraisal* of results achieved and their correlation to attributes are necessary. Appropriate counselling needs to be done to overcome weaknesses and to exploit the strengths for achieving better performance. The progress made should be monitored on a continuous basis and counselling done as and when required. Conflicts will inevitably arise when individuals work together; more so, because one of the management principles entails the audit of the work of one department by another. For example, the quality control department checks the incoming material procured by the purchase department. The organisational work ethos should encourage the resolving of problems at colleague level or peer level. However, in case of continued disagreement, the authority for deciding should be specifically designated. Therefore, clear-cut, updated organisational charts, supported by delegated authority levels, are required.

2. The wisest and safest method to resolve a disagreement between two parties is to set a joint task. During the completion of the task, an interface should be created in order to foster emotional bonds. Differing views should be tested out and a solution evolved. However, if the task poses a challenge to each party to disprove the other, a sticky situation may arise; leaders would need to be sensitive to this dimension of the problem.

3. Innovativeness and creativity flourish best in an atmosphere of challenge. Competition – domestic and international – poses the greatest challenge. The challenge lies in keeping ahead and increasing the lead on an ongoing basis, and finally winning the race. The organisation may be providing goods or services or both. Such a situation will call for creating/identifying new customer needs, new product/service improvement methods, new product/service development and adding value for the customer. Speed is important for keeping ahead in the globalised business environment; however, unplanned haste can lead to disaster; it is an inescapable necessity to keep the competitors' activities/achievements in focus all the time.

4. The losers invariably get hurt. Their 'pride' and concept of 'self-worth' are adversely affected. Managers must cultivate amongst themselves and in others an ethos in which winning or losing is not a matter of individual accomplishment; in fact, what is right and best for the organisation should be done. Creativity in, and an innovative approach to, problem-solving can result in a win-win situation, where both parties see the fairness of results and save their faces.

5. Temper or anger is a very strong human emotion. An angry person tends to become irrational and takes decisions which may have adverse long-term implications. Organisations need to impart training in self-awareness, through available validated behavioural techniques. Such inputs generate understanding of one's own behaviour and can lead to self-improvement. A short-tempered 'boss' can put off his subordinates; he neither gets full details of failures nor receives any worthwhile suggestions. Such an eventuality erodes the concept of synergy and is dysfunctional for the organisation.

NUGGETS

- Management of conflicts should result in what is best for the organisation.
- Survival is assured for innovative/creative organisations.
- Self-awareness can be taught in order to facilitate an individual's development.

25. Ganesha and the Moon
(The Ancient Story)

1. Once, Ganesha was out riding on his rat. Suddenly a snake came in the way. The terrified rat abruptly jumped and threw Ganesha off. The moon saw how Ganesha fell and laughed loudly. Ganesha got angry and punished the moon by breaking one of his tusks and throwing it at the moon. The moon soon lost its light and disappeared.

2. Both the gods and the common people became very worried by this happening and prayed to Ganesha to forgive the moon. Meanwhile, the moon also realised its mistake and asked for forgiveness from Ganesha.

3. Ganesha was ultimately pacified, but to teach a permanent lesson to the moon, he decreed that during the first fifteen days of every month, the moon would get bigger, and then become smaller for the next fifteen days. At the month's end, the moon would look like Ganesha's tusk. Finally, it would altogether disappear, and then again become gradually bigger.

1. Managers generally select their mode of conveyance, clothes, office machines and decor on the basis of individual values, status and likes/dislikes. At times, they may appear incongruous to others. However, they have the right to choose whatever they are comfortable with. Powerful people can be generous and are expected to control their baser emotions like anger, greed and malice. However, they are also human. At times powerful 'bosses' can get into difficult moods and to laugh at them or criticise them or comment against them can make them angry and vindictive. They could mark out those who have offended them, for punishment, which is meted out when a suitable opportunity arises. When angry, punishment much harsher than deserved may be inflicted. At such moments, the powerful can act irrationally, without considering the long-term implications. If the provocation is grave enough, even those managers, generally known to be calm and collected, can get terribly upset.

2. The punishment meted out to a senior person in an organisation serves as a reminder to others to desist from dysfunctional behaviour. At times the use of the 'stick' is essential, since providing 'carrots' all the time leads to loose discipline. The punishment should make the guilty feel repentant and want to modify their wrong behaviour. The effect is not restricted to the guilty person, but also extends to that person's seniors, on-par colleagues and subordinates. Admitting the mistake, seeking forgiveness and assuring the authorities that it will not be repeated in the future provide the best way out for the errant person.

3. Total forgiveness for a mistake committed generates a sense of complacency towards target achievement among the employees. The feeling that they develop is: 'whether I produce results or not, the management will not punish me or does not have the guts to punish me.' In such a situation the work ethos gets distorted and individuals get a feeling that they can get away with any lapse. Also, excess laxity damages management credibility, because for a long time, the management has maintained that dysfunctional behaviour will result in punishment, and when something goes wrong, it fails to take specific punitive action. The severity of the punishment may be reduced, by modifying it, but some action *must* be taken against the guilty so as to serve as a reminder for all others in the organisation. Moreover, it helps establish the management's image of being firm, fair and yet human.

NUGGETS

- Employees must desist from making uncalled-for comments against the seniors.
- Errant behaviour deserves punishment; it is not the severity but the certainty of punishment which corrects the behaviour.
- Punishment, when meted out, must be tinged with a humane approach.

26. Chintamani – The Wish-Granting Jewel
(The Ancient Story)

1. Kana was a cruel prince. He troubled everyone; even the gods and sages. Once, when out hunting, he came to the ashram of Sage Kapila.

2. Sage Kapila welcomed Kana and expressed his desire to serve a meal to the prince and his followers. The prince looked at the simple cottage with a thatched roof and wondered how the sage could feed them all. The sage had a sparkling jewel, which he wore around his neck. He prayed to the jewel and at once countless delicious dishes and drinks appeared in a beautifully decorated hall. All guests were suitably served. The jewel had been given as a gift to Sage Kapila by Lord Indra. The jewel was called *Chintamani*. Kana asked Sage Kapila for the jewel, saying that the needs of a king would be better served by the wish-granting jewel, rather than those of a hermit, who had few needs. Kapila refused to give the jewel and so Kana took it away by force. Sage Kapila became very unhappy. He prayed to Ganesha for long years; Ganesha was finally pleased and decided to punish Kana.

3. Kana had a dream that the sage was coming with an army to get back his jewel. Kana decided to immediately prepare for war and kill the sage. Kana's father tried to stop him, but failed. The army of Kana marched towards the ashram of Sage Kapila. The forces of Ganesha defeated Kana's army and Kana himself was killed. *Chintamani* was thereafter restored to the sage.

The Related Modern Management Concepts

1. Managers are appointed to work for the specific good of the organisation in particular and society in general. They are given certain powers to facilitate the achievement of the targets/goals set for them. One of the primary tasks of a manager is to build a competent, cohesive team, involving his seniors, on-par colleagues and subordinates, so that, each team member contributes substantially to the achievement of overall goals. Some managers with inflated egos and drunk with power adopt a highly dictatorial style of functioning. Each one of their interactions with others is seen as an opportunity to demonstrate their great power and belittle others. Such autocratic behaviour is adverse to effective organisational working.

---

2. Every organisation has certain confidential material/information with respect to product design, manufacturing process, conceptual knowledge or manual skills. This information must be zealously guarded and shared only with the limited loyal few and efforts made to stop it from falling into the competitors' hands. The availability and location of confidential material/information, if disclosed to the wrong-thinking persons, immediately increase chances of its loss. Vested interests would make all efforts to obtain such information for their selfish use. The means resorted to would normally be unfair.

---

3. Once lost, the retrieval of the original or making good the adverse impact on the organisation is a long and painful process. The wrong-doer was obviously smarter and/or stronger than the original owner; otherwise the theft attempt would have been foiled. The original owner would then need to identify an ally, who agrees to help. The ally must be such that their joint knowledge and power are adequate to defeat the wrong-doer. Consequently, the organisation should be security conscious and remain alert at all times.

NUGGETS

- Managers who exploit employees can achieve results over short periods only.
- Organisational secrets which are the basis for its survival and growth must be zealously guarded.
- Organisations must strengthen themselves through linkages with reliable 'allies'.

27. The God of Fire (Agni) Gets Angry
(The Ancient Story)

1. Agni, the god of fire, resided on the earth, along with other gods. He was very kind by temperament. He helped human beings even in the simplest and smallest of jobs. Because of this trait, Agni was not liked by the other gods.

2. It once happened that the gods and demons attacked each other and fought a long war in order to win control over heaven. Agni contributed considerably in helping the gods to achieve victory. The other gods moved into heaven and celebrated their victory. In doing so, they forgot to take Agni with them, who was left behind on the earth.

3. Agni was very upset and decided to teach the other gods a lesson. He made flames and smoke burst out and choke the doors of heaven; visibility became very poor and the eyes of the gods started to burn.

4. The gods in heaven realised their grave error and sought the forgiveness of Agni. They were shown the error of their ways and made to sing praises of Agni. The matter was thus peacefully resolved.

1. In every facet of life, a human being needs support and help; be it related to the job, family or society. The simplest and smallest of activities or tasks, if left unattended due to pressures of life, can result in major problems. Leaders and managers should remain alert to the needs of their employees and provide help or counselling whenever and wherever the need is felt. Such leaders and managers may be wrongly perceived by their bosses and peers as soft or overkind, but, in reality, they may not be so.

2. Under adverse conditions, the seemingly weak unfold their total potential. However, they continue to keep a low profile and, at times, are overlooked. The top management must establish an objective, fair and visible method of evaluating the contribution of all the employees and also ensure that no person in the organisation gets left out, especially in the sharing of success and joy.

3. Employees who do not get due recognition become emotionally upset. Being overlooked once may be explained to the employees (who are upset), but a string of such unfortunate events can compel the individuals to adopt a militant stance, leading to adverse implications such as loss of productivity, strikes, and *gheraos*, which could have been avoided.

4. When things begin to go wrong, the sensible managers need to initiate action rapidly and with an open mind. Acceptance of their error and re-emphasising the individual's contribution go a long way in countering the damage. Very often the personal 'ego' of the manager hinders objective decision-making. Such a predicament can be avoided by using the following formula: 'Look for *what* is right, not *who* is right.'

NUGGETS

● An objective evaluation of the contribution of each team member is essential.
● The distribution of rewards should be fair and equitable.
● The courage to accept one's own mistake is essential.

---

28. Sage Kanva
(The Ancient Story)

1. Sage Kanva had two wives and both were talented and wise. One wife was a Brahmin who bore him a son named Megatithi. The other wife belonged to a low caste (Shudra) and bore him a son named Trishak.

2. Megatithi was arrogant because of being a Brahmin. During a quarrel he belittled Trishak, stating that the latter would not be able to acquire the knowledge of the Vedas, as he was not a Brahmin.

3. Trishak challenged Megatithi to a competition, to determine which of them was greater. Each had to walk on fire. Trishak emerged successful and unharmed, while Megatithi's body started burning. Megatithi, however, refused to accept defeat, saying the fire (Agni) being a god, refused to touch Trishak because he was a Shudra. Trishak suggested that they should swim through the big river as a test for identifying the better person. Trishak then came out dry and untouched, but Megatithi became thoroughly wet. Once again, Megatithi refused to accept defeat, saying that the river was pious, and hence would not touch the low-born. A third competition was then agreed upon, to see who could sing better and attract a larger number of cows. Trishak was able to attract a large number of cows, while Megatithi could not attract even a single cow.

4. Megatithi finally conceded defeat and decided to increase his knowledge. He decided to learn how to sing and attract cows. It took Megatithi one year of dedicated hard work to compose a song to be able to attract cows. Eventually, Megatithi became a better person.

The Related Modern Management Concepts

1. The wise and competent managers should not be guided by parochial tendencies engendered by religion, caste or race. They should develop relationships on the basis of the qualities of the individual. Being born of high caste or low caste does not necessarily elevate or degrade one's qualities, conduct and achievement, which give a comparative placement in life.

2. Arrogance born out of parentage or caste is harmful; children of managing directors/owners are not necessarily clever. They have an advantage as far as material requirements and educational facilities are concerned, but need to earn their place in life through a display of intelligence and competence. The sensitive and wise persons evaluate the relative strengths of others and befriend them for the organisational good.

3 (a). Interdepartmental or interpersonal rivalries are destructive and adverse to organisational interests. A lot of time, energy and thought is wasted in playing games of one-upmanship, i.e., proving how one is better than the others. If allowed to remain unchecked, such games lead from one unproductive incident to another. The top management must discipline the deviant and undertake team-building measures to develop a productive culture.

3 (b). Introspection by managers is essential; it helps them identify their relative merits as individuals. Also, it allows them to see 'what is right' and accept the higher level of knowledge/skill/competence of others. Thus armed, they can apply individual strengths for the organisational good.

3 (c). The head of any organisation must instil in all the department heads the ability to appreciate the importance of their functions and also of the interdependence they have on other functions, in order to generate mutual respect, harmony and team spirit amongst the members. Remaining alert to any deviation and correcting it quickly is essential, before matters go out of hand.

3 (d). Competitors must not be underestimated. It would not be possible to win against them unless one evaluates their strengths and weaknesses correctly, as also the business opportunities and threats. Winning is meaningful through developing relative strengths over others, rather than playing on their weaknesses.

4. An ongoing system of self-evaluation is necessary for all leaders/individuals in respect of their function/department. Continuous training to keep abreast of current developments/ situations/requirements must be provided. New knowledge, skills and abilities needed must be identified. Self-development has to be planned and carried out with total dedication so that future success is ensured.

NUGGETS

- Competence is not directly related to parentage.
- Internal conflicts call for urgent remedial actions.
- Personal success results from continuous self-development.

29. The Narsinh Avtaar
(The Ancient Story)

1. King Hiranya Kashyapu decided to take revenge when he learnt that Lord Vishnu had killed his brother. Therefore, he decided to please Lord Brahma with his devotion and seek a boon of indestructibility. The king spent long years praying to Lord Brahma. At last Brahma was pleased and granted a boon that no man or beast, nor any weapon would kill him either at night or day, inside the house or out of it. The king became proud and started harassing even the gods. Anyone taking the name of Lord Vishnu in his kingdom was severely punished.

2. Prahlad, the king's son, was a great devotee of Lord Vishnu. This angered the king and he started troubling his son. As a result, Prahlad was, on different occasions, pushed into the fire, thrown into the sea and dropped from a mountain top, but each time he survived, being protected by god. One day, on being asked, Prahlad told the king that Lord Vishnu was everywhere, even in the column of the palace building. The king broke open the column and Vishnu (the preserver) appeared in the form of Narsinh (half man, half lion, i.e., neither beast, nor man). Narsinh had a lion's head and paws; the king was killed in the evening (neither day nor night), while Narsinh sat on the threshold (i.e., neither inside the house nor outside). Narsinh used only nails to tear open the stomach of the king thus no weapon was used. Thus, not only was the boon granted by Lord Brahma honoured but also Hiranya Kashyapu was killed, by adopting a novel approach.

1. Despite the passage of time, a large number of conflicts continue to remain alive, because the wronged parties, in reality or in imagination, wish to take revenge upon each other, thus creating a vicious circle. People hurt others, at times knowingly, to teach them a lesson and, at other times, because they lack correct understanding of the other person's stand. At times, managers are called upon to take ruthless decisions in the long-term interests of the organisation. Every ruthless decision will be easier to accept if the situation at the moment of committing the act is objectively anlaysed, shared openly and discussed rationally. The delegation of any power, to any person, is never absolute. Whenever power is misused, its effect can last only for a while, since employees are bound to confront it someday, more so, the talented ones. Competitors will either 'pirate' the dissatisfied talent or use them as 'in-house informants' to obtain confidential information.

2. Owners/managers at times get drunk on the 'power' they enjoy. They develop wrong ideas about their self-importance and self-worth and consider themselves as infallible. Whoever expresses dissent or disagreement with their views is harassed, punished and, at times, made to leave the organisation. Allowing dissent to be expressed openly, in a constructive manner and finding innovative solutions taking into account differing views, are now seen as increasingly important management tools for organisational development. Ruthless curbing of dissent turns 'thinking' human beings into 'plain, mechanical doers', who invariably fail whenever the environment changes and calls for new approaches. 'Power-drunk' managers start living in a world of make-believe; they cannot see the reality and become complacent. Lack of such alertness and not maintaining a continuous lookout for possible threats, particularly new ones, lead them into darkness. Competitors will take advantage of this situation by adopting novel and innovative approaches. Eventually, the 'power-drunk' fall from their lofty positions and leave the organisation badly bruised and humiliated

---

NUGGETS

- The attitude to reach an amicable settlement is more fruitful than purely seeking revenge.
- One should use power for organisational good and not for one's own 'ego massage'.

30. Lord Brahma and the Two Bags
(The Ancient Story)

1. Lord Brahma, the creator, having created man, felt obliged to ascertain whether he was happy or not and what more did he wish for. Consequently, Lord Brahma called man and questioned him about his desires. Man expressed his wish for enjoying peace, health, wealth and appreciation from others.

2. Lord Brahma then handed over two bags to man. The first bag contained the vices of all other beings and the second one those of man himself. Man was instructed to hang the first bag on his back (neither to be seen nor shown) and the second in front, which man was to see and show to other beings. However, man, by mistake, reversed the bags; he hung the second one on the back and first one in front. Therefore, man kept seeing and showing the vices of all other beings. This generated anger in other beings against man. Instead of development, this led to man going downhill.

3. Man got confused when the boons given by Lord Brahma did not result in fulfilment of his desires. Man sought out Lord Brahma and pleaded for such fulfilment. Lord Brahma pointed out the mistake committed by man. Having realised his error, man reversed the order in which the bags were hung and soon started enjoying peace, prosperity and happiness.

1. The entrepreneurs, owners or professional chief executives/ managing directors are accountable, in all respects, for the organisations that they own or build up. Their attitudes, their ways of thinking, their value systems and their conduct should reflect the magnitude of the accountability they carry. A globalised economy generates tremendous pressures for an organisation while trying to remain ahead of competition and gearing up to meet future challenges; the buck finally stops at the top man's table. However, the top man must not get isolated in an 'ivory tower' and should not remain cut off from his people across the board. The top man always receives processed information through his immediate subordinates; the colour and tone imparted during the processing of raw data depends on the competence, personal values/biases and 'political' tendencies/ aspirations of the subordinate. To become aware of the 'organisational reality', the top man must see things for himself, both on the production floor and in the offices. Unscheduled random interactions with the line and staff members will give a feel of the organisation's pulse to the top man. However, such interactions must be totally devoid of any intention to give direct orders, short-circuit intermediate management levels or use the information so received as a device to punish the subordinates; any such behaviour will prove highly dysfunctional.

2. Instructions given to subordinates must be clear and specific. It is also essential to pass down the logic of the decision to the individuals so that they can initiate remedial action on their own; otherwise all problems are conveniently delegated upwards. Such a situation is acceptable in a monopoly market, for a short duration, but, in the long run, every employee should be a contributor to make the organisation strong. One should always remember that *'a chain is only* *as strong as its weakest link'*. Subordinates become better equipped to deal with unforeseen situations, provided the 'boss' and his top-level team discuss with them the possible outcomes of a decision or action. This appears to be a time-consuming/wasteful activity in the short run, but proves productive in the long run.

3. The 'boss' should be accessible when the subordinates need him, both physically and attitudinally. That mistakes will be committed when people work is a fact that the boss must accept, as also the fact that mistakes generate negative learning (what *not* to do), but do prove useful, all the same. The boss must use such opportunities to train his people, so that the mistakes are not repeated. 'Management of mistakes' by itself is a topic of management learning.

NUGGETS

- Managerial accountability with respect to results is an inescapable burden.
- Logic imparted along with any decision taken facilitates subsequent goal achievement.
- The 'boss' must be trained in the management of mistakes.

Part V

Sikhism

31. Guru Nanak: His Langar
(The Ancient Story)

1. After his travels, Guru Nanak returned to Kartarpur in A.D. 1531. The Guru spent his time in communion with god and also in prayers and teaching.

2. A distinctive feature at Kartarpur was the Guru's free kitchen (*langar*). It provided not only good palatable food but also equality for all those who came — rich or poor. This tradition continues even now.

3. A large number of devotees visited the Guru, day and night. The Guru spoke to them about the golden rules of religion, morality and code of conduct and behaviour.

4. Guru Nanak himself worked in the fields like a farmer. His followers, called Sikhs, lived a simple life as a happy family. Some worked in the fields, some cooked, some brought provisions and some served in the *langar*, thus meeting the needs of the persons who stayed with or visited the Guru.

1. All human beings are aware of the existence of a power greater than that of the mortals – the name given to such a power by individuals is an outcome of birth, education and choice. This power provides an anchor in times of adversity, difficulty and trouble. Logically, therefore, such a power should be remembered in good times also. Industrial organisations also contribute to the veneration of this power by participating in activities such as religious ceremonies and festivities organised by the employees. Their other philanthropic contributions include the construction and maintenance of religious places such as temples or gurdwaras. The top management/managers should participate in all such events, irrespective of their personal choice. Such activities also lead to emotional bonding of the entire team.

2. Food is a basic requirement for each and every human being; it should not only be palatable but also nourishing. In industry, it is not always possible to serve one kind of food for all, since quantity needs of manual and office workers differ; work hours are staggered and, therefore, food timings are different; and the pungency requirement of food has been found to be different for workers, staff and managers. This is a minor situational constraint, as long as the food served is healthy, nutritious, adequate and hygienic. The top management and senior managers should, on a random basis, in rotation, partake of food, snacks and beverages served at different times, as also, see for themselves the administrative arrangements, hygiene, cleanliness, adequacy of servings, and so on. Going around when the employees are eating, with an open mind, can send out messages of genuine caring.

3. The organisational philosophy must be elaborated and practically applied in day-to-day expected conduct and behaviour of the employees. It needs to be continuously repeated for achieving the desired results, for giving rewards (financial and/or non-financial) and for punishing unacceptable deviant behaviour. Such a philosophy should provide role models for others to follow. The behaviour of the top management must be above reproach; setting of such personal examples is essential for nurturing a value-based organisational culture.

---

4. Managers must lead by example; they should not be averse to giving a hand in manual work, if required. They should also update their competence to guide their subordinates; this would be possible only if they keep in regular touch with new processes, machines, instruments, gauges, systems and gadgets. Simple, clean living among one's people should be insisted upon. Too much of wall-building is detrimental to the exercise of the 'personal charisma' of the leader whose presence should not be felt only through notices, circulars or memos, but by being seen physically. Work must be allocated to different groups and team members in clear, specific terms. This would mean the maintaining of an updated organisation chart; laying down job descriptions; identifying key result areas; setting personal targets; and, above all, monitoring of performance, to meet organisational goals. All these factors are essential for success.

NUGGETS

- Organisations must meet basic human needs appropriately.
- Managers must lead from the front and not be averse to performing manual tasks.

32. Guru Nanak and Bhai Lalo
(The Ancient Story)

1. During his travels, Guru Nanak once spent some time living with his friend, Bhai Lalo, who was a carpenter.

2. In the same town lived a rich man named Malik Bhago. While Guru Nanak was staying with Bhai Lalo, Malik Bhago invited all the locals for a feast. Guru Nanak was also invited, but he did not attend the feast. Bhago got angry and ordered his men to bring Guru Nanak. On being asked by Bhago as to why he did not come, Guru Nanak explained that he only took food which had been obtained after honest labour. Guru Nanak further elaborated that he would not eat any food purchased by the wealth of Malik Bhago since it had been amassed by cruel means. Then Guru Nanak asked Malik Bhago to bring his sweets and sent Lalo to bring his coarse bread. He squeezed both of them; one in each hand. Milk flowed out of the coarse bread of Lalo and blood from the sweets of Malik Bhago.

1. The top management should perceive the true worth of people and only then make friends. Such 'true friends' are very few and very rare. Such people must be respected and kept close to the heart. Factors such as affluence, riches, outward sophistication and conceptual abilities are not prerequisites for genuine friendship. Business realities call for developing a large circle of acquaintances and contacts; however, all of them will be motivated by their own self-interest and it would be wrong to treat them as genuine friends. There is always a need for real friends to whom one can turn for balanced, unselfish advice, more so when one is caught in a dilemma.

2. Prosperity is generated in an organisation by the combined efforts of each team member. In industry, the sharing of this prosperity forms a major issue between the top management and other team members. Employees come to work and expect fair emoluments for their effort. Organisations exploiting the employees in a cruel and unfair manner tend to suffer from violent backlashes one day or the other. In the long run the owners themselves have to pay for such misdeeds. The philosophy for generating continuing profits should be by sharing equitably, duly rewarding the employees' contribution, and ploughing back a part of the profits for future growth.

NUGGETS

- Real friends, genuinely wanting the best for the organisation, come in different garbs.
- Exploitation of the weak leads to short-term profits only.

33. Guru Nanak and the Sacred Thread Ceremony
(The Ancient Story)

1. At the age of ten, Guru Nanak was required to go through a religious ceremony and wear the sacred thread known as 'Yagyo Paveet'. Hardayal, the family priest, was requested to come and perform the ceremony.

2. Guru Nanak asked Hardayal about the importance of the sacred thread, but did not receive a satisfactory answer. Then Guru Nanak explained that everyone should get the thread of contentment from the cotton of work coupled with compassion. This thread should be given twists of truth and ties of self-control. This is the real *sacred thread*, which the spirit needs. This thread shall neither break nor get soiled. It will neither burn nor get worn out. Blessed is the man who goes with this thread on his person.

The Related Modern Management Concepts

1. Organisations are made up of human beings. Of all the resources at the management's disposal, human beings are the catalytic agents who produce the desired goods and services. Organisations should propound their philosophy (a belief system) enshrining human dimensions so that the organisational objective rises above the sole aim of making money. This belief system acts as a motivator for performance; a beacon for conduct; and a guide when faced with difficult decisions involving moral values. The belief system must not be allowed to degrade itself to an empty and meaningless ritual. The logic/value behind the beliefs should be imparted such that it gets internalised by each individual for application; open forum discussions should be held from time to time, so that grey areas, if any, can be clarified.

2. Teams are built to achieve goals. Goals must have a visible component of a missionary facet, so that once accepted by all, they bind the team together. This commitment to a higher purpose leads people to voluntarily sacrifice their personal interest for the organisational good and in support of their colleagues. The managements must plan, organise, execute and monitor all actions, events and thrusts such that, each individual and every team

(a) derive contentment and satisfaction from the job;

(b) keep human values in mind during decision-making, i.e., even when compelled to take ruthless decisions, the task is done in a manner that the person is not hurt and does not carry a permanent scar (in the form of a grudge);

(c) honour truth in practice; at times statements/actions would need to be put across in a tactful manner, wherein the message gets across but antagonism does not result

and the transaction should result in a win-win situation
for both parties;

(d) maintain self-control at all levels; a sense of accountability
for results, commitment to approved code of conduct and
the desire to rise above momentary temptations must
be included in the work environment.

NUGGETS

- Management beliefs are useful only as long as
  people understand and apply them practically.
- Teams excel only when the targets encompass a
  higher, noble purpose.

34. Guru Ram Das Appoints Guru Arjan Dev
(The Ancient Story)

1. When Guru Ram Das (one of the Sikh Gurus) felt that his stay on this earth was coming to an end, he decided to choose his successor. Guru Ram Das carried out a number of tests before deciding that his younger son Arjan Dev would be appointed as the next Guru, and not his elder son Prithia. He shared this decision with other senior Sikhs and obtained their agreement. Guru Arjan Dev was appointed as the next Guru, in a traditional ceremony.

2. Prithia expressed his anger and dissatisfaction to his father for having overlooked his claim as the elder. Guru Ram Das counselled Prithia not to get angry and to accept his decision like an obedient son. However, Prithia did not heed his father's advice.

3. After Guru Ram Das left this earth, Prithia declared himself as the Guru and succeeded in gathering some Sikh followers. Prithia and his followers created all kinds of difficulties for Guru Arjan Dev. However, Guru Arjan Dev remained calm, happy and contented throughout the difficult times. In due course Guru Arjan Dev was accepted by all as the real Guru.

1. In industry, generally, management succession is not given its due importance. The more senior the person, the greater is that person's area of accountability/responsibility. A vacancy can be caused through retirement or an unforeseen accident: the former event is predictable, but is consciously ignored because of a sense of immortality or indispensability; and the second event is, of course, unpredictable. However, in either case the vacuum left behind affects the organisation adversely. The question then arises: why suffer avoidable pain and loss? Identification and grooming of successors to become managers at all levels must become an ongoing activity, especially for those who occupy senior and critical jobs, which will vary from one situation to another. The additional benefit is that no employee can hold the organisation to ransom. The decisions taken in the context of succession must be ratified by impartial panels at appropriate levels in order to avoid subsequent manipulation and politicisation. This will also facilitate planning of suitable management development inputs and counselling to improve weak areas.

2. Identification of suitable individuals and subsequently placing their names on promotion panels need to be carefully planned activities. The job profile and the person profile for the next likely assignment need to be clearly spelt out. The strengths and competence along with the shortcomings must be listed down after careful testing and evaluation of demonstrated performance. Such individuals must then be trained over a period of time, not only in technical fields but also in behavioural and general management and in attitudinal areas. One of the methods is to let them bear the responsibility for a higher assignment for short periods at a time; e.g., when the boss proceeds on leave/sabbatical/ long tour/training programmes. Too long an apprenticeship undergone by the successor under the same senior can be dysfunctional, since it may freeze the thinking of the junior in the mould of the senior. Personal attachments and sentiments will play a part in any selection process. However, their adverse impact can be reduced by data-based evaluation. Team members should be consulted, since they have to support the new incumbent and help him succeed. The psychological commitment from selection panel members to the promotees is automatic, since they are a party to the decision-making process.

---

3. It is but natural for those superseded to feel hurt and express their anger and resentment against the management. Very often such persons make nasty comments and ascribe malicious motives to the people in power. Some regret their statements in their saner moments. However, the more militant ones attract hangers-on and sympathisers to start activities which prove detrimental to organisational interests. Top managements should remain alert to the machinations of such people, counsel them; and, if no improvement is seen, ruthlessly sever their relationship with the organisation. In the ultimate analysis, truth prevails. One of the strengths of managerial character is to stay cool and calm during periods of adversity and hardship. Under such conditions continuing to perform at the highest levels of excellence possible is the only solution. One can draw solace from the saying: 'If night has fallen, dawn cannot be far behind.'

NUGGETS

- Managerial succession plans must exist for all levels.
- Prospective promotees need careful and planned grooming.
- Those working against organisational interests must be counselled; if no improvement takes place in their behaviour, they should be handled firmly.

Part VI

Christianity and Judaism

35. The Buried Treasure
(The Ancient Story)

Jesus Christ once recounted a story as follows:

1. One day a farmer was walking on a path in a field. His foot struck against a piece of iron sticking out in the path. The farmer was hurt. He decided to remove the iron piece, lest it hurt his family members, who would come to the field later, or the labourers he had hired to help him during harvesting. The farmer tried to pull out the iron piece but did not succeed. He then used his spade to dig a hole around the iron piece; eventually, it needed a lot of effort and time to dig a big enough pit. He cleared all the soil, and to his surprise, found a buried chest. On opening it, he found a large number of ornaments and jewels. For long years he had planned and dreamt of how he would use the wealth that he came to generate/acquire to meet the needs of his family and his own self. He exchanged the treasure for the field and thus achieved his life's ambition to acquire assets and become self-sustaining as a family.

2. Jesus drew some lessons from this story. At times you come across treasures of wisdom and knowledge purely by chance. You should appreciate their value, since they are a divine gift; they can help you realise the ambitions of your life.

1. Managers do face difficulties and obstacles in the job situation – some of them hurt their feelings or emotions or ego, or else adversely effect further progress towards their goal. Such blockages must be evaluated objectively. The attitude should be one of removing them in self-interest and for the sake of others who may also come across them. In achieving one's goal, *adhoc* efforts usually end in failure. Problem-solving should be done on the basis of data collected, collated and analysed. Correct machines, tools and instruments are needed to achieve success, and their availability and appropriate usage need to be ensured. Problem-solving involves both time and effort. The complexity of the problem is directly proportional to the time and effort required. Success in the job situation equates itself to effective self-development, viz., knowledge and its application; building up correct values, beliefs and attitudes; generating productive and harmonious interpersonal relations; contributing to excellence in organisational performance; being creative in product improvement/new product development; and finding solutions to complex situations. To achieve success it is essential to conceptualise the need for self-development, plan for it, monitor progress and initiate remedial measures as and when needed.

2. Elders, who possess knowledge and wisdom, tender advice and counsel which lead to definite success. In the industrial world, where all people are not morally upright and trustworthy, individuals must evaluate the elders in their own manner, prior to taking their advice unquestioningly. Objective evaluation should not be based on *what* the elders say, but on the *results* of their conduct and behaviour. The knowledge and advice given (by the elders), once tested, should then be applied to real-life situations.

NUGGETS

- An objective analysis of various problems and the usage of correct methods or tools/instruments for solving them leads to success.
- Individuals must first evaluate and only then act on the advice given by others.

36. A Parable
(The Ancient Story)

Jesus once recounted a parable:

1. A farmer, while sowing his field, spread the seeds far and wide. He wanted to cover every inch of his land.

2. Some seeds fell on the open path which ran alongside the field. The birds saw the exposed seeds and took them away.

3. Some other seeds fell on stony patches. Lack of soil prevented the seeds from developing strong roots; they grew for a while and then died.

4. Still other seeds fell among the thick bushes growing near the outer edge of the field. They grew for a while; however, the stronger bushes and weeds captured almost all the sunlight and nutrients and this killed the freshly growing grain plants.

5. The remaining seeds fell on healthy soil and grew into strong plants. The farmer provided adequate water and manure and the plants yielded an excellent harvest to the farmer of many hundred times of grain compared to the quantity of seed he had sown.

6. Jesus interpreted this parable to his disciples, explaining to them that all seeds have the potential to grow and yield harvests, but it is important that they be sown in the right place and in a favourable environment; otherwise they would be wasted.

The Related Modern Management Concepts

1. The top managers need to pass on their knowledge, attitudes, code of conduct and values to every employee in the organisation. Every employee wants to achieve growth and success; the opportunity to learn and perform must be made available to every individual. Organisations tend to undertake management development and training for those who appear to be high-flyers. In this process, very often, individuals with dormant potential get left out and it is the organisation which stands to lose.

2. Trials, tribulations and failures in life tend to leave employees with hardened attitudes; this is particularly so for long-serving employees who have not grown along with the organisation. Such persons tend to flock together. They get caught in a vicious circle, and the fear of being treated as deviant makes them continue with their old behaviour. Managements need to pay special attention to such cases and, as a last recourse, ask them to quit.

3. It is the moral responsibility of every leader to nurture young entrants. A youth has 'stars in his eyes', is idealistic and unaware of the harsh realities of organisational life. Leaders need to be sensitive to potentially talented youths and begin grooming them right from the early stages.

4. The placement of young entrants in a particular department/ group should be done very carefully. A group with a record of treating young entrants harshly, and having a large personnel turnover, should be avoided for such placements. Also, a group which has a highly politicised environment should not be entrusted with such responsi-bilities. This is because young entrants get disillusioned with both the work environment and their seniors and feel a sense of stagnation.

In such cases, they adjust themselves to become 'also-rans' or simply leave the organisation.

---

5. Talented people or high-flyers are difficult to attract and retain. Although a large number of people are available in the employment market, persons with 'spark' or talent (demonstrated potential) are few. The talented individuals need to be trained, supported, guided and counselled as part of an ongoing process, till they attain maturity. On reaching this stage, such people become future 'pathfinders', contributors and leaders. To bring them to maturity is relatively simple; to retain them, through the assignment of challenging tasks which continuously stretch their total abilities, needs thorough planning, building emotional bridges and being aware of their aspirations. Achievement-cum-power becomes their major motivator.

NUGGETS

- Placement of young entrants under 'guru-managers' is essential for their appropriate grooming.
- Talented ones are not many; identifying, recruiting and retaining them need managerial maturity.
- The management should ensure that each employee recruited has growth potential; deadwood should not be considered, even temporarily.

37. The Ten Commandments
(The Ancient Story)

1. The Pharaoh (ruler of ancient Egypt), when punished by god, finally agreed to let Moses lead the Israelis, along with all their belongings, out of Egypt across the sea. The Israelis had to face a number of serious situations on their journey to their homeland. The Pharaoh, basically a wicked man, reverted to bad ways and sent his army to destroy the Israelis, once they reached the sea. God, however, made the sea part to let the Israelis pass through, but drowned the Pharaoh's army. In the desert, when the Israelis ran short of food, God sent 'manna' from heaven; when they ran short of water, Moses struck a rock with his staff and a fountain appeared.

2. Once the Israelis were safe, god summoned Moses atop a high mountain. In Moses' absence, his people went back to their wicked ways, forgetting how god had brought them out safely from Egypt. On top of the mountain Moses was given two tablets with the commands of god, called the 'Ten Commandments'. When Moses returned he saw the wrong ways of his people and destroyed the 'golden calf', that was being worshipped, by throwing the tablets at it. God became very angry and wanted to punish the Israelis. Moses pleaded with god and god relented by forgiving the chosen people and giving them two new tablets.

1. Managers need to differentiate among those who commit an error once, those who are repetitively errant but can be corrected, and those who are basically wicked. The first category needs to be corrected softly and duly counselled; the second category should be dealt with firmly and duly counselled till they realise the danger of persisting with their errant behaviour. It is the last category of whom the managers must be most wary. The persons in this category will resort to sweet-talk and make all sorts of promises on being caught, but, at the first opportunity, will revert to their bad ways. Managers must take ruthless action against the basically wicked and ensure their separation from the organisation at the earliest. The punishments must be fair, and based on the philosophy of giving all the possible opportunities and help prior to taking ruthless action. The moral strength which flows from a high value system in the organisation sustains it in difficult situations; such organisations receive unasked for and generous support from both the public and other organisations.

2. Organisations tend to quickly relapse into a euphoria of success, forgetting the lessons learnt from earlier adverse business cycles. Moments of success must be enjoyed and savoured by all employees, but the need for meticulous planning and building of organisational capability to cope with unforeseen future challenges should not be overlooked. During periods of success, adequate resources become available. These resources should be gainfully employed to build up technical competence and cohesive and competent teams, thereby eradicating weaknesses, if any. Success usually gives a distorted image of self-worth and leads to sacrificing of basic value systems – managers and employees tend to become complacent; they overlook value systems; short-circuit working policies/systems; and become overbearing and high-handed. The wise organisations suffer from the trauma of failure only once, and prepare them-selves appropriately for the future, but the not-so-wise go through repeated unpleasant experiences.

NUGGETS

- Repetitive deviant behaviour merits strong remedial action.
- Learning from past traumas should be used for organisational strengthening.
- Credibility of management philosophy increases with the fair and firm handling of deviant behaviour.

38. The Tower of Babel
(The Ancient Story)

1. After the Great Floods, when god had rebuilt the world, Noah was blessed with many children and grandchildren. Over the years, their numbers grew and the grandchildren recalled Noah's words that god would not send down floods again. The people ignored the possibility of god punishing them for their evil deeds in some other way. Safe in their refuge, they took to evil ways and began committing sins.

2. A misguided leader suggested that they all build a tower as high as heaven to show their greatness to god; they had become a proud people. They ignored god and his commands. They all spoke one language and had one goal. The construction of the tower was started and some progress was made.

3. God became angry and replaced that one language with many others. Confusion resulted because communication became near-impossible, since what one said the other did not understand. The people divided themselves into groups, based on the commonality of language. Many groups just moved away and the tower (known as the Tower of Babel) was left incomplete.

1. The entrepreneurs/owners/chief executives who set up a project know the difficulties faced in the initial stages. As the organisation grows, more people from outside join in. The new entrants take existing buildings, products, or facilities for granted; they are hardly aware of the trials and tribulations that the original set of people had to go through, in order to bring the organisation to the current level of profitability. The 'reality' of setting up the project earlier, and another one now, is never adequately impressed upon the employees; they are allowed to live in the present, i.e., in a dream world. Also, the failures/concerns/anxieties of the management are never openly shared with the employees for fear of demotivating them, which is an extremely short-sighted view in that it ignores the fact that the employees are adults and need to be readied psychologically for unforeseen adversities. Employees in a profitable organisation, if left loose and allowed to circumvent policies, systems and procedures, will become instrumental in weakening the organisation.

2. The euphoria of success very often leads to overconfidence and setting unachievable targets. Great enthusiasm is generated by the challenge of starting of a new project and disparate individuals come together to work as a team. Most managements fall into the trap of focussing their entire attention on the technical parameters involved in the construction, installation and commissioning of the project; they neglect team-building, people-related issues and setting up of policies/systems/procedures. Consequently, no sooner has the project gone on stream, such managements are confronted with major people-related problems. Wise managements ensure parallel focus on both these facets.

3. Modern organisations recruit people from different parts of the country, depending on wherever the talent is available; at times, foreign nationals also are inducted. The organisational structure lays down the formal working groups. Within these groups informal subgroups are formed on the basis of factors such as language, caste, customs, religious practices, and commonality of eco-socio-political views. In all organisations both types of groups exist simultaneously. It should be a calculated management thrust to mould the different small groups into one large whole. This becomes possible by practising an avowed philosophy, developing a corporation where people take pride in being its members and where there is no discrimination on the basis of factors such as sex, colour, caste and religion. Communication is an extremely important part of organisational operations; in fact, it is the lifeblood. Managers must generate an open communication climate (upwards, downwards and sideways in the organisation) based on shared values, honesty of purpose, faith and credibility. Given these strengths the growth and profitability of an organisation are assured.

NUGGETS

- Managements must avoid getting caught in the trap of project planning and execution based on gut feelings, hunches and unrealistic assumptions.
- People-related issues must be given equal importance as all other dimensions of a project, from the very beginning.

Sufism

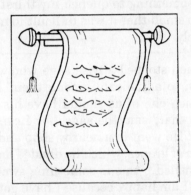

39. The Three Travellers
(The Ancient Story)

1. It once happened that three men decided to go on a journey together. They came upon a small coin by the roadside. As they had no other money, each started to argue with the other two as to what they should buy with it. The first man said, 'I want something sweet to eat!' 'No,' said the second, 'I want lots of sweet things to eat.' 'No!' said the third, 'I want something to quench my thirst.' The value of the coin was so small that it was difficult to meet each one's needs separately.

2. The three men stopped a wise sage who was passing by and asked him to adjudicate among them. 'Choose,' they said, 'as to which one of us should have his desire.' 'I will do better than that,' said the sage, 'for I can undertake to satisfy you all.' He went to a nearby shop and with the coin bought a bunch of grapes, which he divided among the three men. 'I am satisfied – this is something sweet to eat,' said the first man. 'I am happy because I have got a lot of sweet things to eat,' said the second. 'This is something with which to quench my thirst, and so my need is met' said the third man. The sage was able to satisfy not only the individual but also able to keep the group together.

1. Conflicting demands for resources are always voiced by different functions/departments in an organisation. This is a natural phenomenon. Every manager examines the task entrusted to him and evaluates the resources required. Availability of resources in full measure makes task achievement easy, because it reduces the effort needed to somehow make-do. A safety cushion is built into the demand for resources, to offset the adverse impact of any cut imposed by the seniors. This aspect needs to be understood as the reality. Dynamic, energetic, growth-oriented and wise managements are always confronted with the inadequacy of resources with respect to one or some of the four M's (men, machines, money and materials) and two T's (time and technology). Therefore, they develop creative and worthwhile strategies to achieve the task by using limited resources.

2. Creativity in management lies in finding solutions which meet the demands of all concerned optimally. This entails in-depth understanding of all functions; developing an ability to evaluate each demand objectively; and putting them together into a cohesive whole. A specific thrust area for management development is building up of an innovative/ creative environment, more so, in a globalised economy. Arriving at fair and equitable solutions which will satisfy every department/function is not easy; the greater difficulty arises in convincing them individually and, as a whole, that the solution arrived at is the best. Once the teams and subteams genuinely accept the decision, they would put in their best efforts for achieving the targets. Such a situation reduces, if not eliminates, subsequent politicised manipulations – a big gain for the organisation.

NUGGETS

- Unlimited resources are never available. Creative solutions are needed to utilize the limited resources optimally.
- Resource allocation must be fair and equitable.
- The management should share the logic to convince all persons of the fairness of allocation.

40. The Abandoned Building
(The Ancient Story)

1. A group of Bahaudin's senior disciples, who had been to Persia, had arrived to sit at the feet of the master. As soon as they were assembled, Bahaudin ordered them to listen to tales and poems narrated and recited by the most junior of his followers. The senior disciples appeared cynical and upset at this turn of events; however, they kept quiet.

2. Then the master said: 'If you follow this track for half a day's march, you will come upon a beautiful, abandoned building. You will see that one side of the magnificent dome is covered with moss. If you enter the building you will find that some of the precious tiles have slipped, and lie on the floor. About the value and grandeur of the building, there is no doubt. But exposure to certain human shortcomings and natural elements has caused a loss of perfection. So it is with the senior disciples.'

1. The youth and inexperience of the new entrants into an organisation have a positive side also. Factors such as their level of conceptual abilities, willingness to learn, manual skills, positive attitude towards building interpersonal relationships, social mingling, a fresh awareness of life and their personal aspirations are different from those of the senior managers. The youths view issues, problems, events and people from their unique point of view; thus they are able to provide a more objective view and suggest innovative approaches. Very often the senior managers are not inclined to hear them (the youth) out; discuss matters; and adopt creative ways, because the fear of failure, and of being ridiculed, is very high in most old-timers. The senior managers, having succeeded by following a particular approach, are averse to changing themselves even though the environment has changed. The older organisations suffer greatly because of this rigidity of thought and perception among the senior decision-makers. Managements must ensure that 'fossilised thinking' is not allowed to set in.

2. The entrepreneur who created/started a successful organisation deserves full credit and appreciation; such achievement cannot be played down or treated with scant respect. However, the organisation is subject to the effects of external forces of competition, the dynamics of the business environment and social/economic/political events. The top management must be alert to all these factors and take appropriate steps to counter them. In addition, periodic evaluation of internal strengths and weaknesses of the organisation must be undertaken. The human element (i.e., every employee) should contribute to exploit the strengths and reduce the weaknesses so that, through constant renewal, the organisation remains a success story. Timely

remedial action to correct small weaknesses will avoid the
need for a painful protracted organisational turn-around
later on.

NUGGETS
● Managers should use the special attributes of the young for strengthening the organisation.
● Planned efforts are needed to avoid rigidity of thinking in senior managers.

41. The Key Spot
(The Ancient Story)

1. Dhun-Nun, the Egyptian, explained graphically in a parable how he extracted knowledge concealed in an inscription on a Pharaoh's statue. This statue had a pointing finger, upon which was inscribed: 'Strike on this spot for treasure.' Its origin was unknown, but generations of people had hammered the place marked by the sign. Because it was made of the hardest stone, little impression was made on it, and the meaning remained cryptic.

2. One day, Dhun-Nun, engrossed in contemplation of the statue, observed exactly at midday that the shadow of the pointing finger, unnoticed for centuries, followed a line in the paving beneath the statue. Marking the place where the shadow stopped, he obtained the necessary tools and carefully removed the stones. The removal of the stones brought to light a trapdoor which led to a cave below. Going into the cave, he found beautiful articles reflecting superb workmanship. Dhun-Nun was thrilled at having acquired such priceless treasures. He was able to dispose them off, collect large sums of money, and thus meet all his material needs.

1. The work ethos in an organisation needs to be created such that individuals seek in-depth knowledge, and do not accept superficiality as reality. Decisions based on superficial thought and analysis are bound to be second-rate. It is important not to rush into an activity, following the first idea that comes to the mind. Deliberation is important. This calls for management development in areas of decision-making, based on hard-core data collection, collation and analysis. Managers/department heads must periodically review the performance against targets set, in order to determine whether any changes in strategy are necessary.

2. Problems tend to acquire an image of being 'too complex to be solved', especially after a number of people have tried and failed. The solution to such long-standing problems needs peace, quiet, concentration, dedication and perseverance; above all, it demands acute observation and analysis and a creative approach. Top managements must identify individuals with talent and provide them all facilities to come up with creative solutions to add to organisational strengths. For achieving results, organisations need to provide good 'tools of the trade', as appropriate, to their people. Instructions in the correct usage of machines, instruments and the like need to be given, so that the task is completed without damaging either the material or the end product. Innovative thinking brings spectacular results; results once achieved bring prosperity, which all can share.

NUGGETS

- Decision-making must be a deliberate and well-thought-out activity.
- Intelligent hard work along with innovation is needed for success.

42. The Language Expert and the Dervish
(The Ancient Story)

1. One dark night a dervish happened to be passing by a dry well. He heard a cry for help. He looked down into the well and questioned as to what was the matter?

2. A response came from the depths of the well: 'I am a language expert, and I have unfortunately fallen into the well, since I was ignorant of the path. I cannot come out on my own and need your help'. 'Hold, friend, and I'll fetch a ladder and rope,' replied the dervish. 'One moment, please!' said the language expert. 'Your language and pronunciation are both bad; they need to be improved.' The dervish then retorted: 'If correcting me is so much more important to you than coming out of the well for survival, *you* had better stay where you are till *I* have learned to speak properly.' After that, the dervish went on his way!

1. The human beings working in an organisation must be knit into a team, so that they automatically go to the aid of each other. The emotional bonds that are developed in rendering help when needed are much stronger and longer lasting than those based on formal relationships. Leaders worth their salt do not wait for a cry for help; they are sensitive to people and situations, offering support and cooperation voluntarily. Also, when asked by others, they readily extend help.

2. A thorough knowledge of the path or course to be followed is essential for achieving success. Seniors must show the path clearly by laying down the precise expectations of the management in terms of job description, key result areas and personal targets. They should also 'light the path' by personal example. Advice tendered or help offered must be objectively evaluated for its effectiveness in achieving the desired goal. A display of arrogance and a false sense of 'self-worth', in order to belittle those who come to help, prove dysfunctional. The individuality of each employee must be respected. Having an ego is a universal phenomenon; hurting another person's ego is to turn away a possible friend. Criticising a person who comes to one's aid will leave one friendless.

NUGGETS

- Good team spirit leads to cooperation among the members.
- Uncalled for criticism leads to non-cooperation.

---

43. Team Approach
(The Ancient Story)

1. A lame man walked into a serai (inn) one day, and found a place to sit beside a person already there. 'I shall never be able to reach in time for the Sultan's banquet', he sighed, 'because, due to my being lame I am unable to walk fast enough.' The other man raised his head and said 'I have also been invited, but being blind my progress on the road is very slow.'

2. A wise man who heard them talking said: 'You only need to think and realise that between both of you the means to reach in time for the Sultan's banquet exist. The blind man can walk, with the lame one on his back. Use the feet of the blind man and the eyes of the lame man to achieve your goal.' Thanking the wise man, both followed the instructions and reached in time for the feast; the goal was achieved jointly.

3. On their way, the team of the blind man and lame man stopped to rest at another inn. There they met two other men who were very unhappy. Of these two, one was deaf and the other dumb. They had both been invited to the feast. The dumb one could hear, but was unable to explain to the deaf man. The deaf man could talk but had nothing to say. They missed the feast, since there was no third man to provide them with a solution to work as a team.

1. The management should create a work environment where introspection and obtaining a feedback about one's limitations and strengths and areas for improvement form an ongoing process. This facility becomes available to those who develop strong interpersonal relationships; relationships which are open, objective and aimed at an individual's improvement as part of a team. Awareness of shortcomings is the first step to getting rid of them.

2. Every individual suffers from certain specific limitations. Failure can come to those who operate from a false sense of ego, ascribing to themselves qualities or abilities that they do not really possess and feel it below their dignity to seek advice or help. When help is genuinely needed and asked for, it can come from those sources from where it is the least expected. Team work is essential for success. Shortcomings of one team member are reduced by the strengths of others and so on; the chain becomes strong by each link supporting the other. Team spirit does not fall from heaven; in fact, continuously planned and time-bound effort is needed to generate and sustain such a spirit. Team spirit is based on logic where each one individually and the group as a whole stands to gain. Also, emotions such as empathy, consideration, fellow-feeling and give-and-take play an important role in fostering team spirit. Team work enables a group of ordinary people to achieve extraordinary results. Wise leaders find creative and innovative ways to compensate for shortcomings of individuals in order to achieve organisational goals.

3. Lack of wise leadership dooms an organisation to failure. The resources, though present, are not utilised effectively and are thus wasted. Grumbling about shortage or inadequacy of resources is a favourite pastime of incompetent managers;

the competent ones take matters in their hand, are proactive in attitude and committed to achieving success. Further, the knowledge and experience gained must be shared with or passed on to others who have similar objectives; e.g., employees, customers, suppliers and academic institutions. This requires the organisation to establish meaningful and appropriate communication channels and have a clear idea of the methodology to be adopted in order to win as a team.

NUGGETS

- Individual weaknesses should be compensated by appropriate grouping of team members.
- Ordinary individuals working as a team can achieve extraordinary results.

44. Hasan of Basra
(The Ancient Story)

1. Hasan of Basra describes how he had convinced himself as being a man of humility and humble in thought and conduct towards others. One day while standing on the bank of a river, he saw, at a distance, a man sitting with a flask of wine in his hand and a woman beside him. He thought of the degenerate creature and wanted to reform him.

2. At that moment a boat was seen sinking into the river. The other man immediately jumped into the river and rescued six of the seven people struggling in the water. Then the other man called out to Hasan, saying that if he were a better man, then, in the name of god, save the remaining seventh man. Hasan failed to rescue the seventh man who ultimately drowned. Then the other man informed Hasan that the lady with him was his mother and the wine flask contained only water. He chastised Hasan, who fell at his feet and requested to be saved. The other man prayed to god to save Hasan.

1. Managers, especially the successful ones, should guard against ascribing to themselves qualities and attributes which they may not have, or may have in a measure much less than what they think they have! It is useful to be open to receive feedback about oneself so that a real under-standing of the 'self' exists. Also, one should develop confidants who can be used as sounding boards, in order to check one's own thinking against that of the others. External appearances can be deceptive. To initiate action, without being in possession of full facts, can lead to disastrous results. A false perception can be likened to wearing coloured glasses – all facts get tainted by the colour of the glass and the mind interprets them wrongly to fit into the perception.

2. The competent, who are helpful by nature, do not need to be asked to extend support to those who are in trouble; they do so voluntarily. An ethos of being helpful can be generated in an organisation by appropriately rewarding such behaviour. Such acts and achievements need to be highlighted to others, so that they become guidelines for individual conduct. The arrogant, without requisite qualities, fail when testing times come. However, the guilt of failure and fear of contempt from other team members should be rapidly removed; otherwise such corrosive feelings will eat away the individual potential. Counselling is a managerial responsibility. Counselling helps in explain-ing facts as they are, and also in removing misconceptions held by individuals, more so by those who have failed, since they build up defensive arguments and excuses to justify their behaviour. Individuals will invariably make mistakes – managers after counselling should not hold such incidents permanently against an individual, as long as he does not repeat the wrong behaviour. While counselling, managers must remember that they also carry the burden of their own weaknesses and are not all-powerful – playing god is dangerous!

NUGGETS

- Appearances can be deceptive. Delve deep to reach reality.
- Counsel others to help them improve themselves.

45. Etiquette
(The Ancient Story)

1. An inquirer once asked Sayed Khidr Rumi to identify the best and also the worst of human institutions: Rumi replied: 'Yes, indeed. Its name is *etiquette.*' He further stated: 'Etiquette enables the wise to approach the student without being jeered at and the student to search without appearing ridiculous.'

'The disadvantage of etiquette is that it enables the ignorant to set their own rules of what is permissible in thought and conduct and what is not. This blocks further learning.'

2. The inquirer then asked for an illustration. Rumi replied: 'People, when reading of the doings of the masters feel that it is an analogy which applies only to a stupid man and not to them. *I* could never think like the stupid man in the tale. The reality is that such a person is always the one most in need of teaching, while he is unaware of it.'

'There is the story of the crane who was distressed when a man shouted at him, saying, "Look at that creature with diseased wings!" The crane, instead of looking for a sage who would cure him, jumped into a pool of water and came out dripping wet. He ran up to the man, as if to say, I am OK having had a bath. The man started to curse him even more strongly, because he did not want the crane to shake the water off all over him.

The crane became convinced that the man was irrational, while it was simply a matter of one not understanding the other. In the instance of the acts related to the wise, the student must realise that the sage is talking about a real, not an illusory, improvement in his state.'

1. One of the primary roles of a manager is to manage people. Managing people also involves developing subordinates. By doing so the manager can increasingly delegate responsibility and enlarge their work areas – simultaneously, the manager can take over more responsibilites from his boss. The manager must become adept at acquiring the relevant knowledge, keeping it updated, applying it for achieving results and giving it shape as teaching material. The pitfalls and strengths of the subordinates should be clearly seen, so that all dimensions, both positive and negative, can be included in teaching. The manager, as a teacher, has a relatively easy role with respect to the talented, for they will learn eagerly to better their job prospects. For the manager, the challenge lies in first changing the attitudes of the ignorant towards learning and then imparting knowledge to them. At no stage must the learner feel ridiculed, since that blocks learning – motivation lies in helping the person to build up confidence by being appreciated for the one thing that he has done right, rather than the nine that he has done wrong. This is a slow process, at times frustrating, but the manager must persevere in his efforts.

2. The wise manager looks for genuine growth/improvement in his people for their long-term success, rather than educating them to only discharge their duties for the present. Every individual must undertake objective self-evaluation in order to understand his strengths and weaknesses. This process can be facilitated by obtaining feedback from competent well-wishers who could be the boss, colleagues, subordinates, family members, consultants and the like. Once the areas for improvement have been identified, specific planned efforts should be put in for strengthening them. Those with very strong egos do not accept any feedback; soon enough their well-wishers also stop helping them. Such people continue to give themselves credit for qualities that they do not possess. At the same time, they discredit others who give them sound advice. The pitfall of life is that the talented produce results; success fuels ego; and the talented thus close themselves to self-development and good advice, in preparation for falling flat on their faces one day.

NUGGETS

- The stronger the ego, bigger the block to learning.
- Managers must teach self-evaluation to their subordinates for strengthening the team.
- Managers must accept that their own knowledge can never be complete. Feedback will give them an opportunity to know what further knowledge they must acquire.

46. The Dog Finally Drinks
(The Ancient Story)

The famous Sufi Shibli was once asked:

'Who guided you in the path?'

He replied: 'A dog did. One day I saw him, almost dying of thirst, standing by a pool of water.

Every time he looked into the pool he saw his own reflection in the water and withdrew, because he thought it was another dog.

Finally, such was his necessity, he cast away fear and leapt into the water; immediately the "other dog" vanished.

The dog found that the obstacle (which was himself), the barrier between him and what he sought, melted away.

In this same way my own obstacles vanished, when I understood my real self; covering both minuses and pluses.'

1. Individuals working in organisations generally know their needs, and also, what efforts are required of them to meet management expectations or to develop and grow in their chosen career. Managements innovate to develop and retain employees by (i) drawing up 'succession charts'; (ii) developing training plans; (iii) correlating performance to attributes/knowledge of individuals through performance appraisal systems; (iv) encouraging self-development; (v) sending individuals to management development/skills improvement/behavioural science programmes, and so on. However, finally the individual by himself has to drop his inhibitions and decide to wholeheartedly apply himself to achieve his goals.

2. The leaders have the crucial role of counselling their subordinates. They should help individuals to achieve successes, however small they may be, in order to develop their self-confidence. When individuals make mistakes, they should be treated as learning experiences, rather than as a reason to punish them. The leaders should delegate increasingly complex tasks to subordinates and guide them as and when needed to help them succeed. Subordinates should be given opportunities to attempt new tasks, which they have not tried before. Thus will emerge employees who are self-driven and need no chasing in order to perform and achieve results. Thus each team member will work up to his maximum potential and meaningfully contribute to team success.

NUGGETS

- A burning desire to reach the goal is the best motivator.
- Self-awareness helps overcome false inhibitions.

47. A Strange Agitation
(The Ancient Story)

Once, during a prayer session, a Sufi called Sahl Abdullah went into a state of violent agitation, with uncontrolled physical body movements. Later on, his friend Salim asked Sahl Abdullah as to what caused that state. Sahl replied that this agitation was not, as people imagined, due to power entering him, but on the other hand, was due to his own weakness. Others were confused and asked if that was weakness, what was power? Sahl elaborated that *real power* was acquired through the mental and physical strength of an individual to remain unruffled in times of traumatic adversity.

Leaders are continuously faced with problems, big and small, which need to be satisfactorily resolved. Subordinates observe their leaders in moments of crisis. Accordingly, the leaders' behaviour can motivate or demotivate the subordinates. A leader who loses his sense of balance, or behaves in a flustered or jittery manner in a crisis, tends to make irrational decisions; loses the respect of his team members; upsets them; and ultimately leads them to failure. Leaders who remain calm, composed and clear thinkers and doers in a crisis project their real power and competence. The subordinates feel reassured, gain confidence to tackle adversity, offer total dedication to task achievement and follow the leader to attain success. Leaders gain such power through the acquisition of knowledge and its meaningful application and also by possessing a genuine concern for their team in finding creative solutions to vexatious problems.

NUGGETS

- Leaders must remain calm and collected in times of adversity.
- The leaders' demonstrated behaviour motivates or demotivates the team.

48. The Sheep and the Purse
(The Ancient Story)

1. A shepherd named Asif was walking along a road one day, leading his sheep along with the help of a rope. A thief followed him, cut the rope, and took away the sheep. When Asif realised what had happened, he ran all over the place searching for his sheep. Soon he came to a well, where he saw a man weeping loudly. Asif did not know that the weeping man was none other than the thief. Asif enquired as to what was the matter. The thief replied that he had accidentally dropped his purse, which contained five hundred silver coins, into the well. He promised to pay Asif a hundred silver coins, if he retrieved the purse.

2. Asif thought that when one door closes many others open up. The reward offered was worth ten times the price of the sheep which he had lost. He stripped himself and jumped into the well. The thief made off with Asif's clothes also!

1. In a competitive commercial or industrial environment, rivals are, forever, trying to increase their market share; one way being to take away the market share of others. Globalised and liberalised markets are more fiercely competitive. In today's world the fastest wins the race; therefore, alertness to dangers and staying ahead through diverisfication and innovation offer the right combination for achieving success. The successful entrepreneur who possesses the market leadership attracts trouble; competitors fight him, in the hope of gaining a sizeable market share. During this ongoing struggle, competitors aim to grab the technology, products, finances, infrastructure and, above all, the human resources, mostly the talented ones. The foregoing scenario cautions leaders to remain alert and sensitive to people/situations and not be naïve. The time/form/strategy of attack not being known, the situation calls for continual vigilance.

2. Disgruntled employees can be tempted by competitors to work against organisational interests; such employees can become a source of great danger. A system of checks and balances, involving gathering of information and safeguarding vital data/processes/information is essential for survival in the modern world of business.

NUGGETS

- Beware of competitors at all times.
- Learn to 'read' people thoroughly and know their real worth.
- Avoid complacency at all times.

49. *The Caravanserai*
(The Ancient Story)

Once Khidr Rumi went to the king's palace and made his way right up to the throne. Such was the strangeness of his appearance that none dared stop him.

The king, who was Ibrahim ben Adam, asked him what was he looking for? The visitor replied:

'I am looking for a sleeping place in this caravanserai.'

Ibrahim retorted:

'This is no caravanserai; this is my palace.'

The stranger then asked:

'Whose was it before you?'

'My father's,' replied Ibrahim.

'And before that?'

'My grandfather's'.

'And this place, where people come and go, staying and moving on, what does one call other than a caravanserai?'

Organisations can be considered to be living organisms because it is only humans who manage the various activities. Entrepreneurs and proprietors who treat organisations as their personal property or kingdom are mistaken. They should view their position as an opportunity given to them to lead the organisation to greater heights of profitability, growth, innovation and service to the people/nation, albeit for a limited time. By acting as despots or harsh autocratic leaders such proprietors eventually make the organisation degenerate to ruin in the long run. The philosophy of an organisation must be clearly spelt out and followed by all the employees in true word and spirit. The output may be either goods or services; all persons should struggle to generate total customer satisfaction.

Employees of an organisation are not 'bonded' to it; additions and deletions are a way of life. Individuals will continue to serve if satisfied; if not they would quit. This is more true for those who are highly talented. It is up to the managements to ensure that they develop a climate wherein individuals achieve job satisfaction, take pride in the job and organisation and can grow to their highest potential. Employee stability in such organisations tends to be high.

NUGGETS

- Managements must accept the reality of some fall-out among the talented.
- Leaders can offset the adverse impact of separations by careful managerial succession planning.

50. The Ruler and the Ruled
(The Ancient Story)

A dervish was one asked: 'Which is better, to be a ruler or to be ruled?'

He replied: 'To be ruled. The person being ruled is constantly informed by the ruler that he is wrong, whether he is or not. This gives him a chance to improve by studying himself — for, sometimes, he is indeed wrong.

The administrator, however, almost always imagines that he himself or only his rules and regulations are right; so he has little opportunity to examine his behaviour.

That is why the ruled eventually become rulers, and rulers fall to the status of the ruled.'

He was further asked: 'What then is the purpose of promoting the ruled to status of rulers and the downfall of the rulers to the ruled, as a repetitive process?'

He replied: 'So that rulers may learn what ruling really entails, and the ruled may learn how good, as well as how bad, they really are.'

'But', queried the questioner, 'how can a man have a chance to benefit from this if it takes generations for the ruler to become the ruled and the ruled the ruler?'

The reply was: 'It does not take generations. It happens many times in every man's and every woman's life. The development which you see throughout the generations is simply an illustration of this.'

Most organisations are hierarchical and, therefore, a power relationship exists between the leader and his subordinates. Even in voluntary groups; in social groups; and in other kinds of groups composed of peers, *de facto* leadership emerges. Without a unidirectional thrust being given, goal achievement will not be possible. To obtain or generate consensus, someone has to take the lead for initiating discussions, keeping them in line, recording decisions and monitoring results. The phenomenon of leadership in any group therefore involves a leader and those who accept his leadership.

The leader must objectively assess his subordinates' capabilities; identify their strengths and weaknesses and areas for improvement; correlate their attributes and knowledge to the results produced; and counsel them on methods to improve performance so as to achieve better results. Subordinates accept feedback from competent leaders; especially from those who generate emotional bonds by conduct and behaviour and display a genuine concern for their people. It is then up to the subordinates to undertake self-development to become more effective in their current jobs and prepare for higher responsibilities in the future.

The job of the leader is lonely – he carries the burden for himself and his people. Unless the leader goes in for regular self-introspection and undertakes self-development, he will tend to become inflexible in his thinking. Wide relevant reading of up-to-date literature; seeking and obtaining feedback from competent well-wishers including selected peers/subordinates; and becoming sensitive to people to be able to read their minds, will facilitate self-introspection. This process is an ongoing and continuous one; the leader must set aside a specific time for this activity to ensure that other urgent matters do not distract him from this very important activity. Wisdom/knowledge does not come at fixed times. Every manager must keep an open mind; he should be constantly alert and grab every opportunity, even though fleeting, to learn more and more. Managers must also allocate time to consolidate/update their learning to ensure successful application in achieving the goals and objectives.

NUGGETS

- Every group, to be effective, needs a leader.
- The leader must continuously undertake self-development to retain his primacy in the organisation.

Bibliography

Bhanot, T.R., *Series on Mahabharata*, Dreamland Publications, Delhi, 1992.

Bhanot, T.R., *Series on Ramayana*, Dreamland Publications, Delhi, 1992.

Hemkunt Press, *Stories from Sikh History*, New Delhi, 1971.

Mudholkar, Ramesh, *Anmol Simple Story Books*, Anmol Prakashan, Pune, 1992.

Saxena, Vinay and Arvind, Ambika, *Series on Bible*, Dreamland Publications, Delhi, 1988.

Shah, Idries, *The Way of the Sufi*, Penguin, London, 1968.

Singh, Bhagat, *Shri Guru Nanak Devji*, Young People's Publishing Bureau, Rawalpindi, 1976.

Vasani, T.L., *The Babe of Brindavan and Other Stories*, Gita Publishing House, Pune.